Patterns of Prayer
in the Psalms

Patterns of Prayer in the Psalms

❧ Laurence Dunlop

THE SEABURY PRESS · NEW YORK

Acknowledgments

Exod. 3:3-5; 15:8-9; 19:4-5; 34:6-7; Deut. 9:26-29; Is. 6:1-9; 38:10-11; 40:6; Jer. 4:19; Lam. 2:11; 3:1.2.7-10.19-23.26-33.40-41.55-56.64.66; Ezek. 37:6.9-10; Zech. 9:9; Jonah 4:2-3.8-11; Prov. 3:11-12; Wisd. 13:1-2.6-7; Job 42:1-6; 2 Sam. 12:5-7.13; Pss. 1:2-5; 2:4-7.10-11; 3:5-6; 6:1-7; 7:3-5.8; 8:3-6; 11:2-3; 12:1-2; 15:1; 16:1; 17:3-5; 18:9-15.43-45.50; 19:2.12-13; 20:7-8; 22:1-5.9-11.14-15.26; 23:2; 24:1-2; 25:15-18.21; 26:6-9.13-14; 28:1; 29:1-5.7-10; 30:9; 32:3-5..9-10; 33:4.9; 35.5-9; 38:13-14.17-18; 39:2.3.6.8-9.13; 41:4; 44:9-13.20-22; 45:6-7..16; 46:3-5; 47:3-4; 48:1-2.12-13; 49:7-11.12-13.15; 50:1-4; 51:3-4.8-10.12.16-17; 52:8; 59:4; 60:8-10; 61:2-4; 62:11-12; 63:6-8; 64:7-8; 72:4; 73:1.14-17.21-23.25-26; 74:9; 77:4-6.7-10; 79:5-8; 81:12-16; 83:1-2; 84:1-2; 85:8-9; 86:11; 88:3-5.6.8-15; 93:3; 102:10-12; 103:2-5.8-10; 104:27-28; 105:2.5; 106:4; 107:4.10-11.26-27.43; 108:1.9; 113:6-9; 122:3-5; 124:6-7; 125:1-2; 128:1-4; 130:3-4; 132:1-2; 133:1; 139:13-14; 140:12-13; 143:2; 144:1-2; 145:4-5; Mt. 6:7-9; 11:2-5; 11:28-30; Mk. 14:58; Jn. 3:17-18; 4:21-24; Acts 6:13; 1 Cor. 11:31-32; Gal. 5:22; Heb. 4:12-13; Jas. 1:21-25 are from the Jerusalem Bible, copyright ©1966 by Darton, Longman and Todd, Ltd and Doubleday & Company Inc. Used with permission of the publisher.

Pss. 33:16-17; 40:11-2; 66:6-7; 75:1-7.9-10; 144:5; 149:5-9; Mt. 5:20 are from the Revised Standard Version of the Bible, copyright 1946, 1952 © 1971, 1973.

Ps. 42:5.7.22; 43:5; 137:4 are from The Psalms, A New Translation published by William Collins Sons & Co. Ltd., with permission of the Grail, England.

Other passages are my own translation.

1982
The Seabury Press, Inc.
815 Second Avenue
New York, N.Y. 10017

Printed in the United States of America

Library of Congress Cataloging in Publication Data

Dunlop, Laurence.
    Using the Psalms in prayer.

    Includes index.
    1. Bible. O.T. Psalms—Criticism, interpretation, etc. 2. Prayer. I. Title.
BS1430.2.D85   248.3   81-18441
ISBN 0-8164-2377-6   AACR2

Contents

Note to the Reader

Throughout this book the Psalms are referred to according to the Hebrew numbering, which differs from the Septuagint numbering found in many older liturgical books and especially in older Roman Catholic books on the psalms. The two systems compare as follows:

Greek Septuagint	Hebrew
1-8	1-8
9	9-10
10-112	11-113
113	114-115
114-115	116
116-145	117-146
146-147	147
148-150	148-150.

The numbering of verses counts the first verse of the body of the psalm as verse 1, whereas some liturgical texts and some translations count the title of the psalm as verse 1 or, if it is especially long, as verses 1-2. This should be taken into account if the book is read in conjunction with an edition of the psalms using an alternative method of numbering the psalms or the verses of the psalms.

1✤

Prayer of the Whole Man

Prayer is an affair of the heart.

Modern Westerners are plagued by a sort of dichotomy between head and heart. We tend to see ourselves as a battleground where these two opposing forces struggle for supremacy. Many things conspire to insinuate that the forces of the heart—the chaotic, anarchical, blind forces of emotion—are the enemy. Should they gain the upper hand, all order and constancy would be lost. We would be blown this way and that by forces sometimes tender to the point of being maudlin, sometimes aggressive to the point of being destructive. And so we say one should not let the heart run away with the head. Self-control seems a desirable goal, the self-controlled person being one in whom reason reigns serenely over the unruly and disturbing emotions.

We can look for the roots of this way of thinking in our cultural history. The Greek philosophical tradition, which is at the basis of Western thought, glorified the intellect. For Stoic philosophers the ideal for the human person was to attain "apathy"—to be unmoved by powerful emotion, whether pleasant or unpleasant. Yet the Greeks were also a passionate people who rejoiced in the beauty of the human body as much as they cultivated the mind. The course of Western religious thinking was inevitably influenced by medieval scholasticism, which enthusiastically adopted Greek thought as an ideal way of expressing a Christian view of the world. The scholastics forged a system of thought that was much concerned with discerning unchanging principles underlying the world of constant change that presents itself to unreflective observation. Should we blame them for suggesting to us that the messy, concrete world we live in and react to emotionally can be neglected in favor of an unseen, but preeminently "real" world, accessible only to the intellect? Yet there is a whole world of thought that has escaped from any subservience to scholasticism and yet still chooses to neglect the emotions for the most part as unpredictable, disturbing, and best left out of account. The physical sciences have reigned supreme for a century or so largely by confining their attention to realities that can be measured and controlled exactly. The business world has little place for emotion; one does better by being ruthlessly and coldly efficient.

Our mistrust of emotions is not just something that has been imposed upon us by our cultural or religious heritage. Each of us has a deep-seated suspicion that we would be happier if we could somehow excise or cauterize our emotions. We are particularly vulnerable emotionally. We have at least as many painful as pleasurable emotions, and we all have a stock of humiliating memories of times when our emotions have gotten us into trouble.

Reality outside ourselves touches us emotionally in a raw, unprocessed form. The processes of discursive, logical reasoning present us with reality that is processed. By our reasoning processes we impose a certain order on the chaotic world that confronts us. When confronted by a reality never before experienced, the mind immediately begins to tame this new and "wild" reality; it attempts to categorize, relating this new piece of information with what is already familiar. It cannot, of course, do otherwise. We proceed from the unknown to the known. But once a new piece of experience has been incorporated into our system of thought, put in relationship with what we already know, located within the rational framework which, to us, sufficiently explains the world as we have known it up to this point, it is reduced to submission. It is no longer a wild card in the pack; we can now predict how it will affect the game. And there is a sort of security, an emotional satisfaction, that comes from having things once more under intellectual control. The emotions are closer to the raw material of experience. That raw material sometimes comes across to us as wonderful, beneficent, exciting, desirable. But it can also be threatening, ugly, destructive, and hurtful. We never quite get used to the risk of exposing ourselves to unprocessed experience.

None of us can ever renounce the need to work over, "to make sense of," the data of our experience. But it is possible for us to use the process to narrow down our view of things to the safe and the comfortable. It is possible for us to create a rigid, artificial, and inflexible view of the world and to shut our eyes to anything that refuses to fit within the confines of our system. We are all capable of selective attention; it is one of the devices that enables us to survive and function in a bewilderingly complex world. Every time I drive a car I am running a calculable risk of being killed or maimed in an accident. But because I believe that the extent of the risk is outweighed by the advantages of driving the car, I choose to ignore the risk and put it in some compartment at the back of my mind. If I am wise, it will never slip totally from my consciousness. But to allow it to dominate my consciousness would be equally as destructive of my skill as a driver as would allowing it to be totally forgotten. Similarly, there will be aspects of my experience that form part of the foreground of my mind. Others, while known and acknowledged, will be less central. But I run the risk of losing touch with reality and living inside my head if I allow any element of my consciousness to be totally suppressed.

I will be humanly impoverished if I choose to live completely or principally in the ordered, tamed vision of reality my intellect has built up for me, if I forget that reality is always something bigger than our vision of it. Even the reality of my everyday experience is somehow richer, more colorful than my "processed" vision of it. The real God is to be found in reality. The God I discover in my processed vision of reality could conceivably be an idol I have built up for myself. So I must from time to time take the risk of getting in touch with the reality of things, allowing the wildness of reality to confront and challenge me, reacting and knowing again the splendor of the thunderstorm or the miracle of spring, or the agony of toothache or the pain of loving.

The Greek conception of the human being as composed of two principles—one spiritual, which we habitually call the "soul," and one material, which we habitually call the "body"—was taken over so enthusiastically by Christian thinkers that it stands in most people's minds as the only religiously acceptable way of understanding the phenomenon of the human being. It certainly seems to provide a sound basis for Christian belief in life after death: the soul, being spiritual, is indestructible and capable of the bliss of knowing God as he is. It also tends to make the dichotomy between the spiritual faculty of intellect and the emotions rooted in bodily reactions all the more extreme.

But the human reality is more complex—and richer—than this neat compartmentalization, and there are other ways of doing justice to the mystery of the human being. The "body-soul" model was not the one that most biblical authors used to visualize the human person, and it is certainly foreign to the mentality of the poets responsible for the psalms. Their vision of the human person is relentlessly phenomenological—nothing is postulated about the nature of the person that cannot be observed. Human beings are composed of observable components: flesh, bone, blood, breath, and various organs.

The most basic division is between flesh and bone. The flesh is the soft tissue of the human body, supported as it is by the skeletal bone structure. Each part has its easily observable characteristics. The bone structure is manifestly the most durable part of the human body. The flesh, equally manifestly, is ephemeral, changing. Throughout life our flesh changes. We age. Wrinkles appear. We may get stouter or thinner. And after death our flesh will disintegrate rapidly. Through it all our bone structure remains relatively unchanging. After death our bones will resist decay. The bones, then, are the most durable and "essential" part of the human person. Our deepest convictions are felt "in our bones" (cf. Jer. 20:9). On the other hand, "all flesh is grass, and its beauty like the wild flower's. The grass withers, the flower fades, when the breath of Yahweh blows on them" (Is. 40:6–8).

However, flesh and bone alone do not constitute a fully living human being. Immediately after death, when flesh and bone are still intact, the human person is no longer whole. And, again with appealing directness, Hebrew thought pinpointed the essential difference between the living person and the dead body: obviously in the dead body breath and, less obviously, blood are lacking.

This "breath," which makes all the difference between life and death, is for the Hebrew all one with the mysterious invisible real force that makes its power and action felt in our everyday lives: the wind. In Hebrew, there is but one word for the two realities covered by the words "breath" and "wind" in English: *ruach*. The equivalence of the two is based on a simple observation: breath is—feels like—a little share in the wind. It "blows" through our nostrils and mouth, usually without our giving it any thought, just as the wind blows untrammeled and free through the world. And once that personal share in the wind stops blowing, the human composite is no longer whole—we are reduced to being a corpse that exists rather than a body that lives. Since life is a gift that belongs to God alone, both wind and breath are a gift of God. God breathes the breath of life into man's nostrils, and man becomes a living being (cf. Gen. 2:7). In its untrammeled, free form, the wind is still the "breath of God." One biblical poet pictures the miracle of Exodus, when the wind drove back the waters of the sea to let the Israelites pass, and later caused them to return and engulf the Egyptians who were pursuing them, in these terms:

> A blast from your nostrils and the waters piled high.
>   The waves stood upright like a dyke.
> One breath of yours blew, and the sea closed over them.
>   They sank like lead in the terrible waters. (Ex. 15:8–9)

The breath of life, on which we depend for our vitality, is a constant reminder to human beings of their dependence on God:

> All creatures depend on you
> to feed them throughout the year.
> You provide the food they eat,
> with a generous hand you satisfy their hunger.
> You turn your face away, they suffer,
> You stop their breath, they die and revert to dust.
> You give breath, fresh life begins.
> You keep renewing the world. (Ps. 104:28)

There is something refreshingly concrete about this way of viewing the human being. Our dependence on the God-given wind, which is a cosmic force as well as sustaining our personal life, puts us not only in direct dependence on God who gives or withholds breath, but in relationship with the entire universe, where the same life-force is active. The exhilaration one feels when walking free in the wind, or taking in deep breaths of fresh air, makes utter sense to the Hebrew. We are exposing ourselves, opening ourselves to the life-force of the universe.

The prophet Ezekiel vividly imagines the restoration of the dead to life in a passage (Ezek. 37:1–14) that illustrates the Hebrew conception of the human person. He is commanded to speak the word of God to a valley full of dried-up bones—all that remains, in his vision, of the people of Israel. Not only are the bones devoid of flesh and, even more, lacking the breath of life, they are dry and brittle, and therefore on the way toward that final disintegration into dust which is, barring an extraordinary intervention of God, the destiny of the human composite (cf. Gen. 3:19). It is, however, not beyond the power of God to give life even to these pathetic remnants of humanity, and God's promise is expressed in these terms:

> I am now going to make flesh grow on you, I shall cover you with skin and give you breath, and you will live, and you will learn that I am Yahweh. (Ezek. 37:6)

In a rather bizarre scene, Ezekiel imagines the scattered bones joining together to form complete skeletons, which in turn are covered with sinews before his eyes, and then with skin. But this does not restore them to full human life; "there was no breath in them" (Ezek. 37:8). The breath that will complete the life-giving process is itself a share in the wind:

> Say to the breath: "Come from the four winds, breath; breathe on these dead, let them live." I prophesied as he had ordered me, and the breath entered them; they came to life again and stood up on their feet, a great, an immense army. (Ezek. 37:9–10)

This vital force, which is common to all living beings (even the animals—cf. Eccles. 3:21), is not possessed by all in an undifferentiated way. The Hebrew is aware that different human beings live at different levels of vitality. Particularly vital individuals share in the "breath" or the "wind" in a peculiar way. In English religious language we introduce a different word here to express the special endowment of an outstandingly gifted person. We speak of such a person as possessing a special gift of the "spirit." Here again our language can mask from us a striking unity of thought that is found in Hebrew, which, for "spirit" uses the same word as it uses for "breath" and "wind": *ruach*. The highly gifted person has a particularly intense share in the breath common to all.

Sometimes this results in a strikingly vivid way of seeing and imagining events. Thus when Samson performs incredible feats of strength and violence, he is described as being "seized by the Spirit (or the "breath" or "wind") of God" (cf. Judg. 14:6; 15:14). Giving these words the full concrete force they possess in Hebrew, we get an image of Samson gulping in air before these feats of strength, much in the fashion of a weight lifter or a karate expert. He is seized and strengthened by the life-force of the universe, the breath of God.

But the breath of God does not always produce manifestations of brute force. It can also seize upon a man and make him prophesy. Description of the early bands of prophets ascribe to the breath of God the power to snatch a person into ecstasy. This process can be aided by, or at least prepared for by, such aids as music and dancing. Saul is instructed to seek out a group of prophets in 1 Samuel 10:5–6 and submit to the contagion of the enthusiasm that is moving them:

> As you come to the town you will meet a group of prophets coming down from the high place, headed by harp, tambourine, flute and lyre; they will be in ecstasy. Then the breath of Yahweh will seize on you, and you will go into ecstasy with them and be changed into another man. When these signs are fulfilled for you, act as occasion serves, for God is with you.

Again this is a vivid picture, suggesting exalted mental states accompanied by frenzied breathing and heightened awareness. The esteem for such exalted states, which sees them as times when God is especially close and communicates in a special way, is something of an affront to our esteem for the coolly rational. Scholars have often been at pains to stress that the picture painted here is one of a primitive stage in the development of prophecy, and to absolve the prophets whose works are preserved in the bible from any suspicion of such undignified and irrational behavior. But must we really suppose that the rational, controlled, cerebral approach esteemed by the scholars really puts us more immediately in touch with the mysteries of life and the universe than abandoning oneself to a greater force? There is enough in all branches of religious tradition to favor the a-rational and supra-rational, and to suggest that human persons who limit their perceptions to what they can attain by discursive reasoning are choosing to walk when they could be running.

Special gifts of the spirit or breath of God are, however, not confined to such ecstatic manifestations. The artisans entrusted with the construction of the ark of God and the appurtenances of worship are also especially gifted with breath:

> Yahweh has singled out Bezalel, son of Uri, son of Hur, of the tribe of Judah. He has filled him with the breath of God and endowed him with skill and perception for every kind of craft, for the art of designing and working in gold and silver and bronze, for the cutting of stones to be set, for carving in wood, for every kind of craft. . . . (Ex. 35:30–35)

The breath, the wind, or the spirit, then, make the difference between life and death. There are so many degrees of sharing in life that one can hardly begin to enumerate them all. Sharing in life puts one in touch with the cosmic force that brooded over the waters at the beginning of God's creation (cf. Gen. 1:2). God's action in man is always one with his creative activity in the universe. The extent of our submission to this divinely active breath measures the extent to which we rise above the level of "surviving" to the level of "living."

Just as the importance of the breath or the wind or the spirit in the Hebrew conception of the human composite is based on simple, not to say naive, observation, so with the Hebrew reverence for blood. Here the point of departure is somewhat different. One can easily observe that loss of blood weakens the body or that animal-life ebbs away with the blood and, in extreme cases, loss of blood causes death. Hence the simple conclusion, in the words of Leviticus 17:11: "the life of the flesh is in the blood." Even in the light of this reasoning it is perhaps more difficult for us to empathize with this special reverence for blood than it is to feel something of the mystic reverence for the breath-wind-spirit. However, the strange power of blood over the human psyche still manifests itself—there are still people who faint at the sight of blood!

This reverence for blood is the basis for certain Jewish laws and customs, notably the abhorrence for eating blood, and the use of blood in ceremonies of cleansing and consecration. Since blood contains life, it is sacred and belongs to God. It may not be put to profane use, and above all can never be eaten (cf. Gen. 9:4–6; Deut. 12:23–26). Sacred as it is, it communicates something of this sacredness to anything it touches. Hence part of the ceremony constituting Israel as Yahweh's people, a "kingdom of priests, a consecrated nation" (cf. Ex. 19:6) consists in pouring blood on the people (Ex. 24:8). When Aaron and his sons are set aside for special priestly tasks, they are anointed with blood (Lev. 8:23). Cleansing involves a sort of reconsecration to God, and hence can also be effected by anointing with blood. At the great Day of Atonement the *kapporeth*, the throne of God, is smeared with blood, thus cleansed of the defilement caused by the people's sins and made again a fit place for God's presence (Lev. 16). The ritual for sacrifice always involves bleeding the animal to be offered and pouring out its blood before the altar. This is not an offering of the blood to Yahweh; it is already his and man is therefore not competent to offer it to him. The flesh of the animal is man's to treat as he wishes (cf. Deut. 12), and so can be offered back to God. The blood was never man's in the first place, and this fact is acknowledged by his refraining from offering it; it is simply poured out.

The feeling for the sacredness of blood was so deeply ingrained that at the time of Christianity's first diffusion among the pagans it was laid down by the council of Jerusalem as one of the few prescriptions of the mosaic law that the gentiles should observe out of respect for the feelings of their Jewish brothers (cf. Acts. 15:29). It also explains much Christian language about the efficacy of the blood of Christ.

Flesh, bone, blood, and breath are the important components of the living human being. One could, of course, make a still more extensive catalogue. We saw that Ezekiel mentioned sinews and skin. However, the four elements mentioned above are the significant ones in the Hebrew and therefore the psalmists' conception of man. But the human being functions through various organs, and some of these are important enough to merit special consideration.

One of the very significant ones is the *nephesh*, usually translated into English as the "soul," which we then proceed to understand according to the simplified Greek model of man as the spiritual principle in the human composite. The word had a far earthier, tangible meaning for the Hebrews literally, "throat." How then did it come to be so strangely translated as "soul," and how did the throat come to play such an important role in the Hebrew conception of man? The answer to the latter of these questions gives us an answer to the former.

For the Hebrew, the throat is the organ of hunger and thirst.

Hunger, thirst, taste, satiation, are all "felt" in the throat, and since these are the most basic and earthy human experiences of longing, the "throat" comes to be regarded as the organ of all experiences of longing, even of longing for God. Psalm 62:1 speaks of the *nephesh* waiting for God; Psalm 63:1 speaks of the *nephesh* thirsting for God like a dry weary land; Psalm 42:1 compares the longing of the psalmist's *nephesh* with the panting of the doe for water. Since we tend to consider the longing for God as a "spiritual" thing, in which the soul is active and the body plays no part at all, we naturally tend to locate such a spiritual longing in the soul. Hence for centuries Western man, formed by Greek thought, has understood "*nephesh*" in the psalms to mean "soul." He has thereby lost something of the concreteness, the earthiness, the vividness of the psalmists' imagery.

The second organ of prime importance in the psalmists' anthropology is the "heart" (in Hebrew *leb* or *lᵉbab*). The modern Western imagination also gives a good deal of importance to a person's heart. We speak often of the human heart, and our languages are full of idiomatic phrases that reflect the central importance we accord to the heart. This is not simply because of the undeniable physiological importance of the heart, about which we are so much more informed than the psalmists ever were. For us still the heart is something more than a muscular pump that drives our blood around in our bodies and so plays a vital role in oxygenating our bodies. We think of it as the organ of emotion and this, like all popular notions, is rooted in human experience. Violent emotion produces felt responses in our heart—we are aware of it "jumping" with excitement, or constricting with fear, and so on. On the other hand, we know that our brain is the organ of thought, and this organ is not so skittish as the heart. Our brain does not usually give us the impression that it is "leaping"—or anything else much. If we are subject to headaches it is not easy to tell what causes them—the brain does not react so quickly or evidently to stimulus as does the heart. If we have the good fortune not to be subject to headaches, our brain never reminds us of its existence. And perhaps this encourages us to consider our thought processes as rather serene and mechanical, and decidedly spiritual, out of reach of the grosser kinds of physical stimulus. And we can very easily picture a dichotomy between our head (cool, unruffled), and our foolish, unstable heart.

For the Hebrews there was no such dichotomy. For them the heart was the organ of thought. Solomon was a man of great wisdom. He could "talk about plants from the cedar in Lebanon to the hyssop growing on the wall; he could talk of animals and birds and reptiles and fish. Men from all nations came to hear Solomon's wisdom" (1 Kings 5:13–14). He is, therefore, a man of "immense wisdom and understanding, and with a heart as vast as the sand on the seashore" (1 Kings 5:9–10). Many emotions were located for the Hebrews in the throat, but they were not unaware of the heart's susceptibility to emotion. Jeremiah exclaims:

> I am in anguish! I writhe with pain!
> Walls of my heart!
> My heart is throbbing!
> I cannot keep quiet,
> for I have heard the trumpet call
> and the cry of war. (Jer. 4:19)

By the very fact that the Hebrews envisaged the thinking process taking place in the heart, which is also moved in emotion, they are perhaps more instinctively aware of the subtle interplay of thought and emotion than we are. This is not to say that we are any the less susceptible to confusing thought and emotion—for all our esteem of rationality, our perceptions and judgments are likely to be a confused amalgam of logical reasoning and blind emotion, and sometimes blind emotion justified by logical reasoning. But the Hebrews are perhaps less likely than we to escape into an abstract world of thought and imagine that it is the whole of reality.

Further, the Hebrews are less likely to split the human person into warring factions—body and soul—the best interests of the one running counter to those of the other. They are not likely to think of salvation in purely spiritual terms, as though God were forced to take sides in the battle within the human person, and had settled in favor of the spiritual. The Hebrews, in fact, envisage salvation in terms that are more concrete. It was unthinkable for them to make the distinction, which comes rather naturally to our minds, between the sacred and the secular. The Hebrew world was material and temporal and at the same time imbued with the divine.

I do not suggest that the Hebrew way of viewing the human person is in all respects better than the Greek-Christian model we have been used to. It made it difficult for them, for example, to envisage a satisfactory life beyond the grave. Probably there is no way of clinching the case for either model, or even for satisfactorily synthesizing the two. The human person is too big a reality and too profound a mystery to be adequately summed up on any one model. But our religious thinking, for so long not just based on but dominated and limited by Greek patterns, can acquire new life and freshness by contact with the Hebrew patterns of thought, by appreciating again the here and now, the immediately present, the world that confronts our senses. Mystics formed in the Greek-Christian tradition have tended to speak of prayer taking place at the "high point" or in the "depths" of the soul. The imagery suggests withdrawal from the everyday world into an ethereal sphere. The psalms are gutsy prayer, the prayer of flesh-and-blood human beings, not of disembodied spirits. Although there are variations of attitude between psalm and psalm, generally speaking they do not invite us to flee the here and now and the world that confronts our senses, but to enter more and more deeply into our immediate experience which will eventually lead us to discover their God.

2 ❊

Prayer and the Emotions

Prayer is an affair of the heart, whether we choose to understand "heart" in the modern Western way, making it the symbol of the emotional and affective side of human nature almost to the exclusion of the rational and intellectual, or especially if we understand "heart" in the richer Hebrew way as the wellspring of human action, the seat of rational operation, but inextricably linked with emotion and affectivity. Either way, prayer is an affair of the heart. It involves human affectivity, the emotional life, in a very real and profound way.

It is striking how frequently Jesus speaks about the human heart, especially in the gospel of Matthew. There we find, on the one hand, that Jesus lays down the most demanding ideals. In Matthew 5–7, the Sermon on the Mount, Jesus claims that something much more thoroughgoing than mere external observance of the law is required of his followers.

> . . . unless your righteousness exceeds that of the scribes and the Pharisees, you will never enter the kingdom of heaven (Mt. 5:20).

This can sound like a new legalism, imposing heavier and more crushing burdens than the old. Yet Jesus will not admit that this is so:

> Come to me, all you who labor and are overburdened, and I will give you rest. Shoulder my yoke and learn from me, for I am gentle and humble in heart. And you will find rest for your souls. Yes, my yoke is easy, and my burden light (Mt. 11:28–30).

This seeming paradox can be resolved by giving attention to the heart as the key to human living. Just as it is "from the heart that evil intentions come: murder, adultery, fornication, theft, perjury, slander" (Mt. 15:19), so the fruitless and destructive in human behavior can be corrected only by a healing of the heart: "Make a tree sound and its fruit will be sound; make a tree rotten, and its fruit will be rotten. . . . for a person's words flow out of what fills the heart. A good person draws good things from that store of goodness, a bad person draws bad things from a store of badness" (Mt. 12:33–34).

Even the most demanding effort is not a burden if we are emotionally and affectively caught up in what we are doing. Human beings regularly impose the most exhausting demands on themselves in the realm of physical exertion and of mental effort, and experience it as fun. They derive from it a satisfaction that is far more than a grim conviction that it is worthwhile. "Their heart is in" what they are doing. A resolution to take more exercise, to eat less, or to give up smoking will be effective only when we discover that these things *feel* good. Living on grim determination does all sorts of damage to the human psyche, robbing us of joy, playfulness, spontaneity, and, ultimately, of energy. It eventually attacks at bodily level as well, in ulcers, hypertension, and all sorts of psychosomatic illnesses.

We need and long for a reconciliation of the forces that threaten to tear us apart. We long for a healing of the heart. This is what Jesus holds out. The kind of healing he proposes is not a slavish, external imitation, it is putting on the "heart" of Christ. Somehow we are to be touched and transformed at that mysterious level which lies below all the divisions and dichotomies we inflict on ourselves.

Our affectivity must be involved in effectively living our ideals, no matter how much simpler it might seem were it otherwise. Well worked out, logical arguments do not necessarily move us to action, no matter how cogent the reasoning may seem. A logically proven truth exercises an influence on a person's life only if it fires the imagination and captures that person by its beauty, so that assent to the truth passes from being a thing of the head to being a thing of the heart. If God's action on human beings is to be effective, it must involve the emotions. Besides, human beings are at their most vulnerable in their emotions; we can be "got at" through them. On the other hand, reason is a stubborn faculty. It is not by accident that a stubborn, self-willed person is described as "headstrong." We are adept at defending our positions intellectually; even lifelong attempts to suppress our emotions do not render us impregnable emotionally.

Even God is bound to respect this law of human nature. He moves us by touching our heart. Scripture abounds in passages suggesting that God's action on the human spirit has an emotional impact. According to John, Jesus' purpose is so that his followers may know joy (Jn. 15:11) and peace (Jn. 14:27). In his famous list of fruits of action of the Spirit, Paul mixes emotions and virtues in a way that is perhaps not altogether haphazard. The fruits of the Spirit, according to Paul (Gal. 5:22) are "love, joy, peace, patience, kindness, goodness, trustfulness, gentleness and self-control."

There has been a strong tendency in Christian spirituality to play down the emotional aspects of love. We have insisted that love resides in the will, not in the emotions. We coined the mindless catch phrase: "You don't have to like people to love them." This is partly a reaction to an unrealistically romantic notion of love that tends to be portrayed in low-quality movies. I suspect that this catch phrase is a way of diminishing the extent of Jesus' demands, so as to make ourselves feel less Christianly inadequate. Further, since our superficial emotions are notoriously unstable, the only way to assure stability in our lives seems to be to make the stubborn intellect the predominant force in our lives. Love is the most basic movement of the human heart. It occurs at a deeper level than any other emotion. It can sometimes be obscured by more superficial emotions and moods, which are capable of sudden change and even startling reversals. It is an emotion nonetheless, and to suppose that it can never or only rarely register in our consciousness is to condemn oneself to an impoverished emotional life. Human beings are immensely inventive in discovering reasons for sparing themselves the risk and pain of loving, and driving love into an inaccessible corner of the human psyche can serve as one of them.

Joy and peace are perhaps more obviously "felt" realities, although even here we can avoid uncomfortable implications of this by a flight into concepts of "supernatural" joy and peace, thus relegating them to a region that lies outside our perception. Certainly Jesus warns that he gives peace "not as the world gives" (Jn. 14:27), and in the Last Supper discourse it is clear that peace and joy are compatible with suffering (Jn. 15:18–27). Like love, the joy and peace that are a gift of the Spirit are not superficial emotions, coming and going with moods. Yet they are emotions. They will sometimes be felt strongly. They will always tend to color and influence our inner lives at all levels.

The other qualities Paul lists, "patience, kindness, goodness, trust-fulness, gentleness, and self-control," are somewhat different. Love, joy, and peace are, of their nature, "felt" realities. Of their nature they tend to surface in our awareness. The others do not necessarily do so. The most desirable kind of patience, for example, is not the sort of virtue that is consciously and sanctimoniously practiced, but one that is so much part of a person that he or she is unconscious of possessing it. This kind of quality flows from the conscious experience of love, joy, and peace. The person who experiences joy and peace is, almost automatically, patient. The person who experiences love for others does not have to work at being kind—it follows as the night the day. The person whose basic experience, not excluding a good deal of surface distress, is of joy and peace tends naturally to be trustful, since he or she has experienced the trustworthiness of life and reality.

Since God is active in our prayer, we can expect to be touched at the level of our hearts. Prayer is not a coldly intellectual exercise, nor something that one undertakes as a duty, expecting to be passive and unmoved by it. To insist, as I want to do, on the place of emotions in prayer is not without danger. It can establish a new legal requirement in our minds: to experience the right emotions. So we become despon-dent and discouraged when nothing seems to be happening to us. Or we become so anxious about whether we are experiencing the right emotions that our anxiety itself becomes an all-absorbing and destruc-tive emotion. Or we set out to whip up the right emotional response in prayer. It may, in fact, be possible for us to whip up a frenzied state of joy or to impose peace when turmoil threatens to take over. These are, however, not God-given gifts and there is something hectic and artificial about them. In the end they may well prove destructive. The healing emotions that are the fruit of God's action are experienced as gifts.

A fruitful approach to prayer lies somewhere between the resigned apathy that comes from expecting that nothing will ever happen at a conscious level during prayer, and the anxiety that comes from feeling that one must force certain emotional responses. Disposing oneself for prayer has been compared by the English Benedictine John Chapman to preparing oneself for sleep. I cannot *make* myself go to sleep. I can only dispose myself for sleep by removing what would drive sleep away—external noise or inner disturbance. It is difficult, though not impossible, to go to sleep in the middle of a busy airport terminal or in the weaving room of a textile mill. It is well-high impossible to go to sleep in the middle of an entertaining show. In seeking to go to sleep we normally put ourselves in circumstances where external stimuli are reduced to a minimum. But even in the most favorable circumstances I will find it impossible to go to sleep if I am unable to let go of the business of the day. If I begin to worry, especially about the difficulty of falling asleep, I shall most certainly not sleep. If I set out to make myself sleep, sleep eludes me. But if I succeed in letting go of all these things, sleep overtakes me. Our intention and expectation will have something to do with the end result, too. Even though it is quite possible, even likely, that the process of unplugging myself from external stimuli and inner activity will induce sleep, it is more likely to produce this result if I go through the process intending to go to sleep and expecting it.

Throughout the above description, for "sleep" we can read "prayer." Just as sleep is a gift, and our contribution to the process of going to sleep is to dispose ourselves to receive it, so with prayer. Chapman tended to presume that since prayer is a "supernatural" reality, it takes place in the "high point" of the soul and will normally not register in our conscious awareness. I would prefer to presume that often, if not usually, once the quieting process has taken place, some movement of the heart that would otherwise not be discernible will become evident. At least it seems that one should approach prayer presuming that this will be the case. These movements of the heart cannot be claimed as though we had any right to them, but because God, in his prodigality, will frequently, or even usually, move the praying person in this way.

Paul said that two such movements are to peace and joy. The former is not just an absence of disturbance, which may be nothing more than a neutral state, but an inner quieting that is accompanied by a sense of awed reverence. The latter goes beyond this, and includes a sort of "lift" of the heart. It can be accompanied by a heightened appreciation of things around us. These experiences can sometimes occur without any evident cause, or they can be associated with some other positive experience. In the latter case, they go beyond the beauty of the experience in a rather baffling way. I may be walking down a tree-shaded path on a summer's evening when suddenly a deep sense of joy and peace breaks in upon me in a way that is more than just an appreciation of the beauty I am experiencing. The experience that has occasioned the breakthrough may be quite familiar to us. We may have walked this path on many other summer evenings without being moved in quite this same way. I could go back the next evening, perhaps even expecting and hoping for a repetition of the experience, and find that it is not there. Such experiences are certainly a movement of the heart. They convey no precise thought content. They are, of their nature, so wholesome and integrating that they cannot but be from God, the source of life and goodness.

Such moments are not reserved for religious people, or people who pray. This we must expect, since God wills that all should be saved and come to the knowledge of the truth (cf. 1 Tim. 2:4), even though it seems manifest that he does not will that all should come to envisage him in exactly the same way or be united in the same external forms of religion. Since they are given, like all divine gifts, as grace, they are not conferred only on persons who deserve them or who understand what is happening to them. But I do believe that they can be much more effective and transforming for the person who recognizes them for what they are, and cherishes them with the reverence which is due to the gift of God. I believe it is possible to grow in sensitivity to and appreciation of such moments, just as it is possible to increase one's enjoyment of music by fostering one's innate feeling for it. Moreover, I believe that, while these moments sometimes break into and force themselves on our consciousness, there are many occasions when the movement is gentler and can be overlooked or ignored. But it is possible to learn from the moments when God obtrudes into our lives a sensitivity to his touch that equips us to attend to and therefore make the most of less powerful experiences of the touch of God.

This last process can be compared to the experience of surfing. Swimmers are lifted by the swell of each wave as it rolls toward the shore. They can ignore the swell and let it pass them by; they can even swim against it or across it. But they can also, when the moment is right, so position themselves as to be carried by the wave farther and faster than they could ever manage by their own efforts. There are two slightly different skills involved. First, the swimmers must recognize, by the *feel* of the wave lifting them, when is the right moment to yield themselves to it. Second, they must know how to let themselves go with it. Less skilled surfers will not always successfully catch the wave, sometimes because they misjudge the point the wave has reached and throw themselves into the wave before it is ready to take them with it, sometimes because, on the verge of throwing themselves into the void with a wall of water about to crash down with them, they lose nerve, refuse to let themselves be carried away, and let the wave pass them by. They will have their chance again, because there will always be another wave, but that particular wave is gone forever. It cannot be recalled.

In prayer analogous skills come into play: recognizing the movement of the Spirit and allowing oneself to be carried away by it.

So far I have talked about emotions that are obviously integrating and exalting. Although one may have some hesitation about deliberately enjoying such moments, lest one fall into a kind of spiritual hedonism, at least it can be argued that they are edifying ("up-building") and therefore at least respectable. However, not all of our emotions are enjoyable to experience, and some can seem impious and destructive. Most of us learned early in life that to express certain of our less "respectable" emotions was not the way to win the approval of those who seemed to have our life and happiness at their disposal. This tends to become a lifelong habit of pretending (to others and, often, to ourselves as well) that such emotions have ceased to be part of our makeup at all. Once we start paying attention to our heart and growing in sensitivity to its movements, we become aware, perhaps with a sinking feeling of hopelessness, that things we had hoped were dead and buried, or at least safely hidden from polite society, are in fact alive and well. Masters of the life of prayer, such as John of the Cross, have long recognized that setting oneself seriously to prayer often seems to unleash a Pandora's box of passions and unruly, unwanted emotions. This is consistent with our reflections: if prayer is an affair of the heart, somewhere in the process of praying the human heart has to be laid open, with its grandeur and its pettiness, its nobility and its nastiness. We cannot be selectively attentive to the movements of our heart. We choose to be aware of all or nothing. But what place can the undignified tangle of emotions other than the "edifying" ones have in our life of prayer?

First, we might reflect with justice that no one promised us a rose garden; no one ever promised that we would always experience God's action in us as pleasant and enjoyable. It is always a continuation of his work of creation and leads to fuller life. The *direction* of his activity is always positive. But part of the process can be a painful dismantling of the unreal structures we have built up in our lives, screening out large areas of reality as part of our defense against the demands of loving and living. The Father prunes branches that bear no fruit (Jn. 15:1–2). The beautitudes list various painful experiences as part of the stuff of happiness: happy are the poor, those who mourn, those who are persecuted (Mt. 5:3,5,10–12). Jesus tells us to take up our cross and follow him, and at least this must mean not to draw back from painful experience. So the mere fact that an experience is painful is no sure sign that it is not from God and doing the work of God. Indeed, we can only avoid suffering by restricting our lives at both ends of the scale, rendering ourselves incapable of the peaks of joy as well as the depths of suffering.

Second, becoming attentive to the action of God within us involves "going into" ourselves, attentively welcoming what we find there. This means that a lot of pain we have chosen to ignore or bury begins to come to our awareness again. We become aware of unruly emotions and upsets that we would otherwise not have allowed to come to the surface. In praying we are vulnerable in a way that we were not before. This is not a pleasant experience, and can be so frightening that we shut down. One of the major obstacles to getting in touch with the healing and integrating action of God in our being is our past experience of the mess we are likely to find once we begin to look within, and our decision therefore to live on the surface. It is only by going *through* these painful emotions that we can arrive at the still point where God touches us.

It is possible to envisage this for ourselves by thinking of human consciousness as a deep well. What occurs at the upper levels is obvious and can scarcely be ignored. But the entire body of water is not moved all of a piece; there can be emotions at surface level that are different from what is going on below. It is possible to experience a certain superficial pleasure, while harboring a pervasive unhappiness at a deeper level. Conversely, it is possible to feel superficially upset, but one's underlying disposition can be one of contentment and even joy. Somewhere in this complex of different levels of experience God is present and active, not, I believe, sometimes or perhaps, but always and certainly. There is a point within us where an integrating and life-giving force is at work. It is there whether we think about it or not, whether we believe it or not. Our lack of attention to it, even our repudiation of it, will not turn it off. But it is worth seeking it out, trying to get in touch with it, even if it does mean getting in touch with a great deal of turmoil as well.

Unless there were some initial experience of peace and joy experienced in prayer, I believe that no one would get involved in a life of intimacy with God at all. Progress in prayer is not meant to lead us away from this initial joy, but deeper and deeper into it. The way to this deeper experience of God's action lies, as I have described, through turmoil and inner suffering. It will also involve the experience of apparent emptiness and lack of discernible emotion. Sometimes masters in prayer seem to suggest that dryness, emptiness, aridity is the point toward which prayer of its nature tends.

John of the Cross, who cannot be accused of painting a rosy picture of the path the praying person can expect to follow, has a more subtle doctrine than this. He expects that the person who lives a prayerful life will be called to leave an initial, obvious, and rather superficial emotional reward in prayer for a more subtle, elusive, but ultimately much more satisfying kind of joy. Upon first acquaintance this latter state is much less exciting and interesting than the former, and one experiences a sense of loss, just as a palate accustomed to spicy, strong-tasting food cannot immediately appreciate the subtleties of more delicate tastes. But if one is content with the new state of things, and accepts its apparent insipidity, one eventually discovers that it is richer, more satisfying and exciting than what went before.

> For the cause of this aridity is that God transfers to the spirit the good things and the strength of the sense, which, since the soul's natural strength and senses are incapable of using them, remain barren, dry and empty. For the sensual part of a man has no capacity for that which is pure spirit, and thus, when it is the spirit that receives the pleasure, the flesh is left without savour and is too weak to perform any action. But the spirit, which all the time is being fed, goes forward in strength, and with more alertness and solicitude than before, in its anxiety not to fail God; and if it is not immediately aware of spiritual sweetness and delight but only of aridity and lack of sweetness, the reason for this is the strangeness of the exchange; for its palate has been

accustomed to those other sensual pleasures upon which its eyes
are still fixed, and, since the spiritual palate is not made ready
or purged for such subtle pleasure, until it finds itself becoming
prepared for it by means of this arid and dark night, it cannot
experience spiritual pleasure and good, but only aridity and lack
of sweetness. . . . (*Dark Night of the Soul*, bk. 1 ch. 11, trans. E.
Allison Peers. London: Burns, Oates, 1952.)

The psalms, being prayer, express a wide range of emotional states,
some joyous and others painful, some respectable, others not. Understanding the psalms requires something more than knowing the meaning of the words or the historical background or date of composition.
It involves some empathy with the experience out of which the psalm
was written. We need to have some awareness of the movements of
our own hearts. By entering into the psalms with this kind of empathy
we may well come to a deeper understanding of the prayer of our own
hearts.

3 ✣

Formulating Prayer

Prayer is an affair of the heart.

The human heart is filled with longings that, at their root, are God-given and intended to be satisfied. Everyone has a longing for absolute goodness, beauty, and truth. St. Augustine expressed it in his famous statement: "You have made us for yourself, O God, and our hearts are restless until they rest in you." Not everyone would identify the object of this desire and longing as God; in fact perhaps most people would identify the object in some more earthy fashion: an honorable position in the world, a bigger house, sex, or human companionship. All of these may be real personal needs, but the nameless longing goes further and transcends them all. The world's oceans are subject to an inexorable tugging that causes the tidal motion of the waters. A mere glance at the sea does not reveal its tidal movement. We immediately see the much more evident motion of the waves or perhaps the bigger movement of currents. But underlying all such movement and ultimately influencing them all is the movement of the tides. The movement toward absolute goodness, beauty, and truth is the tidal motion of the human person. The deeper we look into the human heart the closer we get to this underlying longing, and the purer becomes our understanding of what it is all about.

It is this profound longing that Paul is talking about in Romans 8:22–23:

> We know that the whole of creation has been groaning until now in the pangs of childbirth. And we, too, who are the first-fruits of the Spirit, groan inwardly as we wait for adoption of sons, the setting free of our bodies.

This movement of longing is itself a sort of primal cry to God, which sounds through many, if not all, of our formulated prayers. The eloquence or adequacy of our formulations is not of prime importance:

> The Spirit, too, comes to help us in our weakness; for we do not know how to pray as we ought, but the Spirit himself intercedes for us with sighs too deep for words. And God who searches the human heart knows what the Spirit wants, because the Spirit intercedes for the saints according to the mind of God.
>
> (Rom. 8:26–27)

Prayer is, at its deepest level, not something one has to work at, nor does it come after a complicated learning process. Whether we are aware of it or not, our hearts cry out to God by those inexpressible longings which are in fact our deepest prayer, whether we recognize them as such or not. It is not even necessary that this prayer of the human heart ever come to be correctly formulated in satisfactory human words. It suffices that we allow the Spirit to pray within us. Once again the process of prayer is a process of "going inward" to meet and go along with the prayer that wells up in our hearts. At its deepest level prayer is wordless, but being human we need to attempt to express it.

The human need to express inner states was something that the Hebrews understood very well. Often they express the idea of "meditating," "reflecting" by the word "*galah*," which literally means "to murmur." Thus the Revised Standard Version translates Psalm 1:2 "he *meditates* on God's law day and night," whilst the Jerusalem Bible, more literally, says "he *murmurs* God's law day and night." In fact, the modern custom of reading silently to oneself, and even more the practice of reading by simply scanning the printed word without ever pronouncing the words seems to have been unknown to the ancients. At a much later date, Augustine was astounded to discover that his mentor and guide, St. Ambrose, read by simply forming the words silently with his lips without actually pronouncing them aloud. No one wants to question the undoubted utility of being able to read silently without pronouncing the words to oneself, but it does reinforce our modern tendency to assume that we can do without expressing what is going on inside us. To express externally what is being thought internally gives a degree of reality to our thought that it would not otherwise possess.

"The word" for the Hebrews was primarily the spoken word, and it had for them a very real power. Once spoken it has an independent life and reality of its own. It cannot be revoked. In Genesis 27 Isaac mistakenly grants to Jacob, his younger son, the blessing intended for Esau, the elder. There is no question of taking it back. Esau must be content with a second-rate blessing and is thereby constituted second in rank. In Judges 11 Jephtah vows to sacrifice the first of his household he sets eyes on if he returns victorious from battle. This may have been ill-conceived and unwise, but the protagonists all presume that it cannot be taken back and must run its course, even though the first person Jephtah meets upon his return is his only daughter. A curse lodges in the designated person and will do its destructive work unless something else intervenes. We find it hard not to dismiss such notions as primitive and at least exaggerated. But at least they express a sense of the real power of the spoken word to concretize and give force and effectiveness to what would otherwise remain a nebulous inner reality.

We humans have a need to verbalize and formulate our prayer, steering a middle course between a mechanistic and superstitious view of prayer, where the formula itself acquires a magical power, and a false spiritualization of prayer, to which we modern Westerners are perhaps particularly prone. Jesus, in the introduction to the Lord's Prayer according to Matthew's gospel, perhaps suggests a similar balance:

> In your prayers, do not babble as the pagans do, for they think that by using many words they make themselves heard. Do not be like them; your Father knows that you need before you ask him. So you should pray like this: "Our Father. . . ." (Mt. 6:7–9)

The worth of a prayer is not to be judged by its length or even its eloquence, but by its reality—how true it is to what is really going on in my heart, which is already known to God before I become aware of it myself. Formulating our prayer is not meant to help God become aware of our longings, but it is of real value in enabling us to get in touch with and express for ourselves the longings of our heart.

The closer we get to the source of our prayer, the Spirit moving in our hearts, the more our prayer is in accord with God's will. The closer we get to the wellsprings of our being, the closer we are to the health and wholeness that is always the work of our creator God. Conversely, the more finespun and intellectualized our conception of our needs becomes, the more influence social conditioning and our own personal prejudices will have on their formulation. We need to have a certain critical attitude toward our verbalizations, aware of the split that can develop between our head and our heart once our prayer becomes excessively "heady," once our intellect begins to formulate things the way it thinks they should be rather than listening to and learning from the much less refined but much more immediate and honest emotions.

The psalms, inspired prayers though they be, are not beyond the limitations inherent in any human word. The words are not the reality and they can sometimes distance themselves from the reality they try to express. We need constantly to remind ourselves that the psalms are expressions of basic and universal human longings. Underneath the cultural and time differences that sometimes threaten to create a chasm between us and the authors of the psalms, the longings that we feel are the same as those that drove the psalmists and that they aimed at expressing. Some of the expressions chosen by persons of so long ago may sound strange to our ears; they may even, on occasion, be positively an obstacle to our understanding and appreciation of some psalm or other unless we can see below the surface to the reality expressed. We can only ask ourselves how the meaning we perceive in any particular psalm matches up with the "prayer of the heart" that we become aware of in ourselves as we grow more sensitive to the movements of the Spirit in our own hearts.

Our qualification for understanding the psalms is, at the deepest level, not an expert acquaintance with the languages, customs, and cultures of the ancient Near East. This is useful and enriching and at times can be quite necessary, but it can remain sterile if it is not at the service of the life of prayer.

James 1:21–25 speaks of the use of Scripture as a moral guide that can be applied in an illuminating way to the use of the psalms as a guide and instrument in our own praying:

> Accept and submit to the word which has been planted in you and can save your souls. But you must do what the word tells you, and not just listen to it and deceive yourselves. To listen to the

word and not to obey is like looking at your own features in a mirror and then, after a quick look, going off and forgetting what you looked like. But the man who looks steadily at the perfect law of freedom and makes that his habit—not listening and then forgetting, but actively putting it into practice—will be happy in all he does.

James is speaking of a life-giving and saving word, which can only be the Word of God. He compares it to a seed (it has been planted in you) and to a mirror (studying it is "looking into the law of liberty")—two images that are hardly compatible, but that express two different aspects of the Word of God.

The Word of God is, first and foremost, planted in us. This suggests that it is very much part of us, and to discover it we turn inward, not outward. Though it is so much part of us, we do not necessarily or automatically accept it. If we reject the Word of God in this sense we experience an alienation from our deeper selves, which is painful and self-destructive and must be overcome if we are ever to be made whole. Conversely, even from this point of view alone, to accept the Word of God in us "saves our souls." In the context of prayer, so long as we suppress or deny those profound longings that are of the stuff of prayer, we experience this alienation and division within.

Since the implanted Word is deep within it can, like all that occurs at a very deep level of our being, remain somewhat mysterious to the person experiencing it. It may need the external stimulus of the word of Scripture to come fully to awareness. The Scriptures are written out of their authors' awareness of the Word of God deep within them, and therefore have the power to confront us with an external expression of the Word that we have ourselves heard, but perhaps not recognized, in the depths of our own hearts. When this happens we grasp their content not as some new truth alien to ourselves that we struggle to make our own. It comes with a sort of familiarity, as something we have sensed obscurely all along. We do not just "learn" a truth of this kind, we recognize it. This is an "aha!" experience, the shock and joy of recognition. We do not experience it as the acquisition of truth, as though we had conquered some insight that was reluctant to communicate itself; rather, we experience ourselves as conquered by the truth.

Scripture functions in this kind of experience as a mirror—a mirror that reveals me to myself. Without a mirror my face would be just as it is now, but I would not know it. So the Scriptures reveal the Word of God planted in my heart. They do not create it, but they can serve to make us aware of it and bring it to expression.

This experience can also be expressed in another image: Scripture, the Word of God, is a sword.

> The Word of God is something alive and active; it cuts like any two-edged sword, but more finely. It can slip through the place where the soul is divided from the spirit, or joints from the marrow. It can judge the secret emotions and thoughts. No created thing can hide from him; everything is uncovered and open to the eyes of the one to whom we must give an account of ourselves. (Heb. 4:12–13)

We sometimes experience the scriptural word's power to penetrate, a sort of shock when we sense that our defenses have been pierced and that something we read or hear makes sense to us in a very personal way. It may be a personal challenge that we refuse to face only on pain of denying life itself, or a truth that has suddenly come home to us as self-evident, and that cannot but be part of our outlook from here on in. This sort of experience is possible because there already exists within us the Word of God spoken deep in our hearts. The written word of the Scripture therefore finds in this implanted word a sort of ally, a fifth column. To reject it is to deny our very selves.

As believing Christians, we confess that the Scripture is the Word of God. But not every word of Scripture is God's word *to me* here and now. As a believing Christian, I expose myself to the Word of God, but I need not, and for my own sanity, and ultimately for any of the Scripture to have real meaning for me, I *must* not, suppose that every exhortation, every command, every challenge is addressed to me personally. The Word of God becomes God's word to me when it makes the kind of impact I have been trying to describe, when the objective Word of God resonates with new richness because it finds an echo in the depths of my heart—the "implanted" Word of God. This does not mean that I sift out or neglect those parts of Scripture that do not make this kind of appeal to me. Since my relationship with God is an ongoing thing, and God can and will communicate with me throughout the course of my relationship with him, different parts of Scripture may well "light up" for me at different times. This, too, corresponds to an experience of those who prayerfully reflect on the Scriptures. A very familiar text, one that we have heard many times before, suddenly acquires that new resonance of the Word of God addressed personally to *me*. It becomes really my own.

I have insisted that prayer, to be real, must be "prayer of the heart." Turning to the psalms, it would be fatal to use them as a model to which we must conform, expressing well-defined, approved sentiments that we must arouse in ourselves, and using them in certain approved ways that we must make our own. Rather we should use them as a mirror, as a means of going into our own hearts as deeply as possible and there finding the prayer that the Spirit is inspiring. The psalms lead us into our own hearts and there express for us what is going on. But they do not always lead us to the uttermost depths of our hearts, where we would probably be wordlessly enjoying the touch of God rather than *saying* anything. Something like this is expressed in Psalm 131. But the psalms also express a whole range of other realities that can come to awareness when we look within. It seems to me a mistake to suppose that the psalms always represent the height of prayer. They do not, any more than the individual always lives at the peak of prayer experience. The psalms are not perfect prayers for perfect people. Rather they are inspired prayers for imperfect people, and since this means above all that they are honest, there are times when the imperfection of the person praying is manifested in the prayer.

Not every psalm is for every person all the time. My interior prayer, with which the Spirit gifts me, is not unchanging. There will be times when one psalm takes fire for me, only to be replaced by another when my inner needs change. Perhaps some psalms will never speak for me personally. No matter. At least they will stand as a reminder to me that my own personal experience does not exhaust all the possibilities of human existence, that God may speak to and move others in ways different from the way he speaks to and moves me. Yet I admit this not with a resigned shrug or with a murmured "to each his own." Such psalms also stand as a challenge to go deeper into my inner self and discover if this or that psalm is in fact "not for me," or whether it uncovers levels of my own prayer that I would never, alone and unaided, have succeeded in uncovering.

I may also discover, when I go into myself, that my remaining unmoved by some psalm or other is due to resistances within me blocking such prayer. It is also possible that I experience, not just lack of response to some psalm, but positive repugnance. This can provoke something akin to panic—"This is the inspired Word of God, and I don't like it!" But such moments can be fruitful, too, if I accept the fact of my repugnance with equanimity as yet another revelation of my deeper self. It could simply mean that I am called to a different way of prayer at the moment. We may also react because we reject something of the Word of God to us and therefore something of ourselves. There is nothing that we reject with such violence or loathing as those parts of ourselves that we have somehow come to imagine as ugly or unlovable. In the process, we diminish our openness to accept the Word of God. For example, suspicion of tender emotions can cause us to react violently and negatively to the sensuous tenderness of the Song of Songs. It also limits our awareness of God's love for us, and our ability really to hear the command to "love your neighbor as yourself." The negative reaction we experience can be a precious revelation of an area in which we are deliberately deaf to the Word of God, and of the obstacles we erect to the Word of God.

The discovery of resistances within ourselves to some psalm or other or to some sentiment expressed in a psalm should be taken seriously. It can be the starting point for very personal prayer of the heart. We do not necessarily aim to browbeat ourselves into accepting the sentiment the particular psalm is expressing; it may well be that such is not our prayer at the moment, and it may never be. But it may be a sort of negative guide to the direction in which our prayer is meant to go.

In the consideration of the psalms that follow, I aim very deliberately at using them as a mirror, reflecting on them so as to arrive at a better understanding of that prayer of the heart, which is present in all human persons and accessible to all who reach into themselves to find it. At times it will be necessary to enter into more technical discussion about the meaning of some text or other, or it may even be useful to speculate about the historical circumstances in which a psalm was composed, but it is my hope that this can be kept to a minimum, and always remain subordinate to the main purpose.

4 ❧

Praying from Memory

Memory is one of the basic, influential human faculties. In some respects it can be compared to a tape recorder. It plays on, recording whether we wish it to or not. At times something will trigger the "playback" mechanism and, whether or not we choose it, or whether or not we like it, something of our past is played back to us. Psychological experimenters have shown that nothing is ever really lost in our memory. By artificially stimulating parts of the brain, events which in the normal course of life would never have been recalled can be evoked. Our past is enshrined in our memory.

Many people claim to have "bad memories." By this they mean that they tend to forget appointments, or find it hard to remember faces or names or what they intended to buy at the supermarket. But while the experience of not having some useful information at hand is frustrating, most people have adequate memory of what is vital to them. In fact, it is impossible to forget the really significant things— for good or evil—in our lives. What we cannot remember is generally, in the strictest sense of the word, insignificant—it has no meaning or importance. The fact that we fail to remember is generally a sign that some event did not capture our attention in the first place—it did not present itself as something worth remembering. What I ate for breakfast on the first of May 1953 is lost in the mists of time. It made no deep impression on me and, in the ordinary course of events at least, is irrecoverable. But events that did make a deep impression on me, reaching much farther back into my personal past, are easily available—probably not with dates and times attached, but none the less vividly present.

The ability of memory to sort significant from insignificant events without any real effort is one of its strengths. The archives of a modern public library are overstacked with data about the immediate past, and one of the first tasks of present-day historians will be to work out which events are worth talking about, and which can be left to the anonymity of the unremembered past. Ordinarily our memory does this work for us and, like an efficient secretary, presents us with an edited version of our past, omitting the enormous amount of trivial material and "hitting the high spots."

This does not mean that the work of memory cannot be improved and refined. Any process that goes on in spite of ourselves can be refined and improved once we consciously and deliberately throw ourselves behind the process, giving it permission to operate and carry us wherever it will. Once we begin to do this, and pay attention to what memory has to tell us, we find that it actually contains much more than we imagined.

However, if we compare memory to an efficient secretary, presenting us with a suitably edited version of our past, we can also at times compare it to an overzealous or overdiscreet secretary who, in connivance with various of our fears, may contrive to edit out of our personal history some things that might upset us. Thus it can happen that some highly significant and formative (and painful) events of our lives might be censored by the "erase" button of our memories. But the erasure will not be complete. A gap will remain, and part of ourselves will be obscurely conscious of and concerned about it. Or there may be a sort of unexplained distortion in our image of ourselves that colors our attitudes and ways of coping with life, but can never be pinpointed. If, eventually, we are fortunate enough to recover the missing information, it will be rather like the discovery of a particularly baffling piece that was missing from a jigsaw puzzle, or the discovery of the keystone to an arch we have laboriously but with little success been striving to complete. No matter how painful or even shameful the missing piece may be, we will be more whole and more integrated with it than with an accusing blank in our records.

The ability of the memory to "edit" our past, for good or for ill, means it is not in every respect like a tape recorder. Another important way in which memory differs from a purely mechanical recording device is in its incessant search for a pattern in the events of our life. A first step in this process is its search to match up similar experiences. We are constantly being "reminded of" events of the past. We tend to file similar memories together, to remember constantly recurring sequences. This is part of the ongoing search for meaning in our lives. We do not see the past as a chain of unrelated and meaningless episodes, but as a series of similar events and recurrent patterns. We cannot be quite satisfied with a maverick experience that refuses to fit somehow into the overall pattern. This will remain like a grain of sand in a pearl oyster, a constant irritation that we cannot let go of. Sometimes such an event can eventually be fitted into the pattern we have already discerned in our lives, just as we can sometimes find the place in a jigsaw puzzle for the piece that seemed to never fit. We turn it round and round, and look at it from all sorts of angles, until it becomes clear that it does in fact fit neatly into the existing pattern. We failed at first to see the fit because we did not see it from the right angle. At other times, however, the recalcitrant new piece of information will wreck the old pattern we thought we had discerned, making it necessary to rearrange all the pieces and discover a new pattern altogether.

A third fact about memory, which sets it apart from a purely mechanical process like tape recording, is that it presents us with a past that is subtly changed—we might say at times distorted—in line with our perception of events at the time of their occurrence. Here is a very simple example. I spent part of my childhood living near a small town in the mid-north plains of South Australia. A number of roads meet in the center of the town, and at their junction stands a war memorial in the form of a hemisphere on which the theaters of war in World War I are depicted, and over which there is a cluster of columns supporting a small cone-shaped spire. We left the district when I was eleven, and I did not return for some fifteen years. During all that time the memorial stood out in my mind as the chief feature of the town, and I recalled it as an architectural wonder, rivaling in size and magnificence the dome of St. Peter's. The sequel will be no surprise to you. Upon my return I discovered, with something of a shock, that the memorial I remembered was in fact of very modest size. Even the proportions of its various features were subtly different from what I had remembered. And despite the fact that I know intellectually that my recollection of the structure was rather exaggerated, I cannot shake off the memory completely. My childhood memory of a huge and impressive globe is still much stronger than my rather vague adult experience of the actual memorial.

We could pounce on this sort of experience as proof of the basic unreliability of human memory. We would, we imagine, prefer to get our information from unimpeachably objective sources. But from another point of view, memory is more important than an exact objective record. If I were to write an architectural treatise on the style of war memorials in Australian country towns, I had better do some fieldwork here and now, and base my observations on photographs and recorded measurements. But if I wish to know something of what it was like to live in a town of that kind in the 1940s, I could get more significant information from the memories of individuals who experienced it. My memory of the war memorial is a better guide to the way I experienced it in my childhood than the impression it makes on me as an adult. Memory is, in fact, amazingly accurate, but it records impressions rather than cold, hard facts.

In understanding myself as a person here and now my memory is a precious resource. I have been formed by my memory. My present ways of acting and reacting are influenced more than I imagine by my memories, both for good and for ill. The horse that always shies at the spot where it once experienced hurt is acting out in a very uncomplicated way the sort of influence that memory has on human life in a more subtle and complex way. Good memories set us free to face life confidently and joyously, since we instinctively expect that the future will somehow follow the pattern of the past. Bad memories tend to cripple us, triggering defensive reactions either of withdrawal or aggression.

In all of this I am influenced much more by those stored impressions, which are the stuff of memory, than by the exact record of events. An act of love or concern, let us say, on the part of a parent, which I perceived at the time as an invasion of my rights or as aggression, will live on and influence me in this latter guise, and will therefore be liable to influence my actions in a negative way. To live successfully we do not so much have to live with our *past* as with our *memories*.

For our health of mind and heart a certain amount of healing of memories has to take place. If it occurs, our life experience will gradually mellow us; if it does not occur, our life experience may well embitter us. We need to come to terms with our memory. No other course is open to us. We cannot choose *not* to remember; memory will not be dismissed thus easily and, like all of our basic human equipment, will take savage revenge if it is denied or underestimated. The process of healing may occur to some extent spontaneously, but, again, as conscious and free beings, we are capable of consciously and willingly committing ourselves to this process of healing of memory. We thereby put ourselves in a position to benefit from and further the process more effectively.

We can commit ourselves to this process only if we have an initial faith in the goodness of our lives and the healthfulness of the forces working within them toward integration, peace, and fullness. This faith can deepen and strengthen as we grow in confidence, allowing ourselves to venture into the stream of memory and discovering that we are not overwhelmed or carried away to our destruction. This happens when we discover that the painful and negative side to our memories does not predominate but acquires perspective against the background of the good and positive aspects of our experience. The process can be described in terms used by Carl Rogers to describe his gradual growth in confidence in his own understanding of life:

> Another learning which cost me much to recognize, can be stated in four words. The facts are friendly. . . . It seems to me that I regarded the facts as potential enemies, as possible bearers of disaster. I have perhaps been slow in coming to realize that the facts are *always* friendly. Every bit of evidence one can acquire, in any area, leads one that much closer to what is true. And being closer to the truth can never be a harmful or dangerous, or unsatisfactory thing. (*On Becoming a Person*. Boston: Houghton Mifflin, 1961, p. 25)

Perhaps the ultimate sign of the person in whom this process has proceeded in a satisfactory way is a spirit of thankfulness, a sense that all of it, the good times and the hard times, the successes and the failures, the greatness and the pettiness, has been worthwhile. Those events or features of our life for which we still cannot feel grateful are as yet "unredeemed," and threaten to influence us in a negative and destructive way.

What has been said so far about an individual can be applied, with some modifications, to a community, which has a communal experience and a communal memory. It is very characteristic of Israel that their knowledge of God grows out of their experience and reflection on that experience. The process is summed up in God's words to the people in Exodus 19:4–6:

> You yourselves have seen what I did with the Egyptians, how I carried you on eagle's wings and brought you to myself. From this you know that now, if you obey my voice and hold fast to my covenant, you of all nations shall be my very own, for all the earth is mine. I will make you a kingdom of priests, a consecrated nation.

The starting point of reflection is a fact of their experience: "You yourselves have seen. . ." This experience, rightly understood, leads them to the heart of their reality as God's people: "From this you know. . . ."

The same process is at work in Christian reflection on the life and words of Jesus, from which Christian doctrine about his person comes to be formulated. That process is exemplified in the gospel incident where John the Baptist, imprisoned and, if not disillusioned, at least subjecting himself and his previous assumptions to reappraisal, asks Jesus to explain himself:

> Now John in his prison had heard what Christ was doing, and sent his disciples to ask him: "Are you the one who is to come, or have we got to wait for someone else?" (cf. Mt. 11:2–3)

Jesus gives no direct answer, but challenges John to consider his (Jesus') activity and draw his own conclusions:

> Go back and tell John what you hear and see: the blind see again, and the lame walk, lepers are cleansed and the deaf hear, the dead are raised to life and the good news is proclaimed to the poor, and happy is the man who does not lose faith in me.
> (Mt. 11:4–5)

The answer to the Baptist's question is to be found in what he "hears and sees." God is active in the events of history, and those events are illuminated by reflection in faith on the events. The answer can be discovered only by the questioner. Jesus cannot presume to answer the question for John, though he can warn "happy is the man who does not lose faith in me." To hear the testimony of another person to the significance discovered in events of common experience can be enlightening, but only if it sparks a shock of recognition and discovery in the seeker and illuminates his or her own experience.

Prayerful recollection of the past is a fruitful exercise for both communities and individuals. It serves to keep us in touch with our roots, to help us realize who we are and where we are coming from.

Psalms 105 and 106 are good examples of this kind of prayer, consisting of little more than a prayerful evocation of significant events of Israel's history. In each there is an introductory section calling on hearers to engage in this kind of prayer (Ps. 105:1-5; Ps. 106:1-2). These express in various ways and from various points of view what the psalmist sees as the essence of this kind of prayer.

It is an exercise of memory. The participant is urged to "remember the marvels God has done, his wonder, the judgments from his mouth" (Ps. 105:5); and "Remember his covenant forever" (Ps. 105:8). The vital importance of "remembering" for human living is pointed up in Psalm 106, where the root of a number of famous instances of national apostasy is "forgetting" (cf. Ps. 106:13, 21). It is a proclamation to outsiders of who God is in Psalm 105:1, "Proclaim his deeds to the nations," but is also addressed to God himself: "Sing to him, play to him, tell over all his marvels" in Psalm 105:2.

Reminding God of what he has done seems rather unsophisticated theologically, since God can manifestly not forget. But, illogical as it may be, the Scriptures are not afraid to give space to the human need to remind God of his past deeds, sometimes as a bargaining point with him. For example, when Moses is confronted by the recurrent sinfulness of the people, which threatens to destroy them, he intercedes for them by reminding God of the great deeds he has performed on their behalf:

> Do not destroy your people, your heritage whom in your greatness you redeemed, whom you have brought out of Egypt with your mighty hand. Remember your servants, Abraham, Isaac, and Jacob. Take no notice of this people's stubbornness, their wickedness, and their sin, so that it may not be said in the land from which you brought us: "Yahweh was not able to bring them

> to the land he promised them. It was because he hated them that
> he brought them out, to die in the wilderness." But they are your
> people and your heritage, whom you brought out by your great
> power and your outstretched arm
>
> (Deut. 9:26–29; cf. Ex. 33:11–14).

God's "name" is somehow summed up by a recitation of his deeds
(Ps. 105:3). The name of any being is regarded in the Scriptures as
highly important. A person's being is expressed in his or her name, and
manifested to the world. Since the deepest mystery of God can never
be fully expressed, no one can fully and exhaustively know the name
of God. Even the divinely revealed name "Yahweh" is an expression
above all of the elusiveness and indefinability of God, since it is taken
to signify "I am who I am" (cf. Exod. 3:14). Some approximation of
the name of God can be arrived at not by abstract definition but by
historical record of what God has done. So the name "Yahweh" is so
frequently linked with the recall of his greatest intervention on behalf
of his people by the explanatory phrase "Who brought you out of the
land of Egypt." Hence the recall of God's great deeds is proclamation
of God's name (cf. Ps. 105:1). When Christians pray that God's name
be "hallowed" ("made holy") they are praying for a continuation of
those great deeds that make the greatness of God manifest in the
world.

Psalm 105 envisages this kind of prayerful recall of the past as
having certain effects on the person or persons engaging in it. This
kind of prayer is a form of "seeking God": "Seek Yahweh and his
strength, seek his face untiringly" (Ps. 105:4). By this kind of prayerful
recall the pattern of events emerges, and the action of God in history
becomes manifest. God is known through events, discovered through
his actions.

Where it is real, this discovery has an emotional impact on the
person praying. Psalm 105 expects that the memory of God's deeds
will lead to thankfulness (vs. 1), to "rejoicing" (vs. 3), and to "glorying
in God's name" (vs. 3). The last means literally "praising oneself"
because of the great deeds of God—a sort of self-congratulation expressing deep satisfaction. This joyful and thankful response is the
ultimate aim of the exercise, and the process of recalling the past is
incomplete until it has emerged. We must not strive to manufacture

such emotions, but rather be content to stay with the memory until the experience is complete. There are psalms, such as Psalm 88 or Psalm 89, where the psalmist finds it impossible to reach this stage of completeness about some facet of his or her experience. There is no attempt to cover up the incompleteness in these psalms. The psalmist is left presenting the broken and incomplete experience to God for completion. This is the only appropriate form of prayer so long as the incompleteness remains.

Thanksgiving is important not just because God expects it, as though he needed it to boost his self-esteem. The Scriptures are not afraid to ascribe human emotions to God, and a prophet like Hosea is not afraid to say that infidelity causes God to feel all the hurt of a wronged husband. But if we think that God demands thanks for his benefits just because it makes him feel good, we are denying him the fullness to which even human love can sometimes attain, namely a selfless concern for the good of the person loved.

Thankfulness is a gift for the person experiencing it; it has a mellowing effect upon that person. It adds a dimension to the awareness of the gifted person, who is not only gifted, but filled with a realization of this fact, and an appreciation of it that overflows into thanksgiving. In Luke 17:11–19 ten lepers are cleansed. Most of the stories about Jesus' healings stop there, but in this one one of the ten is moved to return and give thanks. He is the only one pronounced "saved." To a degree, all the lepers were saved, at least from their leprosy. But only one was fully conscious of all that this gift implied, and therefore moved to thankfulness. His cure was completed by awareness and appreciation of what had happened to him.

Psalm 105 recalls a series of glorious events in Israel's history that are obviously matter for thanksgiving: divine protection in the time of nomadic wandering in Canaan (vss. 12–15), Joseph's being sold into slavery and eventually achieving prominence in Egypt (vss. 16–22), Israel's descent into Egypt and eventual escape (vss. 23–39), God's care of the people in the desert (vss. 40–43), and their conquest of the land of Canaan (vss. 44–45). Psalm 106:1–2 still calls upon hearers to thank God, implies that a catalogue of God's triumph is to follow, and that the psalmist will attempt adequately to praise Yahweh. Yet Psalm 106 lists outstanding examples of Israel's sinfulness. Some of the events enumerated are the same as those listed in Psalm 105. Like Psalm 105,

Psalm 106 recalls Exodux (vss. 7–12) and God's feeding of the people in the desert (vss. 13–15), but here the psalmist sees the shadow side of these glorious events; they were not just manifestations of the greatness of God, but revelations of the wickedness of his people. In addition, other unequivocally sin-laden events are recalled like the uprising of Dathan (vss. 16–18; cf. Num. 16–17), the worship of the golden calf at Sinai (vss. 19–22; cf. Exod. 32–34), the refusal of the people to go into the promised land for fear of its inhabitants (vss. 24–27; cf. Num. 13–14), the idolatry of Baal-Peor (vss. 28–31; cf. Num. 20: 2–13), and their failure to exterminate the original inhabitants of Canaan (vss. 34–42; cf. Judg. 2:1–5). Such experience of human sinfulness becomes also an experience of God's faithfulness, and can move the psalmist to pray for rescue from exile (vs. 47). That such events as these can be the object of thanksgiving is an example of the healing of memories that can take place if we let the shadow side of our experience stand and resist the temptation to ignore or suppress painful memories.

Psalm 106:48 is a doxology or expression of praise and thanksgiving to God that was not originally part of the psalm. The psalms are divided more or less arbitrarily into five collections called "books." Each of these books ends in a doxology. Psalm 106:48 marks the end of the third book of psalms. The other doxologies marking the end of a book are in Psalms 41:13; 72:18–19; 89:51b; and 150 (where the whole psalm has the nature of a doxology). It is as though exultation and praise is a kind of matrix against which all other expressions of prayer are to be placed. This in turn suggests that the positive experience of peace, joy, and integration expressed in thanksgiving and praise is the archetypal prayer experience against which all others should be measured.

Psalm 136, after the fashion of Psalm 105, is an act of thanksgiving to God for his mighty deeds, which are enumerated and hailed by the constantly recurring refrain "His love is everlasting!" The "love" celebrated here is one of the very basic qualities of God as discovered in the Old Testament, expressed in the Hebrew word *Hesed*. Something of the content of this word, which is sometimes rendered into English as "mercy," could perhaps be better expressed in the phrase "extravagant love." It expressed the kind of warm-hearted generosity that characterizes the kind of person who will promise the world. In human beings this quality is not often accompanied by the ability to follow through. One learns to discount the promises of such a person, whose generous nature and desire to give pleasure runs away with a sense of what is feasible. In Yahweh this kind of generosity is complemented by another quality, expressed in the Hebrew word *'emet,* which means "fidelity," "faithfulness," "reliability." This is the quality of a person who stands by and follows through on promises. God is therefore a God of *ḥesed wa'emet*—extravagant love coupled with reliability in fulfilling his promises. Yahweh's *'emet* does not mean that he is a predictable God, whose actions have a sort of inevitability about them. The fulfillment of God's promises usually occurs in a breathtakingly unexpected way. Time and again people who rely on God's promises and envisage the way in which they will be fulfilled find themselves looking for fulfillment in the wrong direction. Yet, after the event, one can look back and say, "Yes, God's promises have been fulfilled. I simply wrongly envisaged the way in which they were to be fulfilled."

Psalm 136 does not use the phrase *ḥesed wa'emet,* but expresses the content of that phrase by proclaiming that God's *ḥesed* is everlasting. It is not the changeable, evanescent kind of generosity that human beings often demonstrate. It is a love that lasts. The thanksgiving that is characteristic of prayer from memory is a constant theme in this psalm. Creation (vss. 5–9) is included with the events of Exodus (vss. 10–15) and God's protection of his people during their journey through the desert (vss. 16–23) as motives for praise of Yahweh's *ḥesed.* Consciousness of God as creator is perhaps less basic to Israel's religious consciousness than their realization that he had been constantly active in their history. The moment of creation, of course, is not really present in anyone's memory since, by definition, it preceded any human experience. The fact that creation took place is a projection based on the experience of God present and active in the beauty and majesty of creation—a sense of God in nature, which is the basis for the prayer experience we shall examine in the next chapter.

Psalm 135 also recalls the great deeds of God: his control of the thunderstorm (vs. 7), his discomfiture of Egypt (vss. 8–9), and of the kings whom he dispossessed to make way for Israel in their conquest of the promised land (vss. 10–11). Yahweh's power, manifested in these great deeds, is contrasted with the impotence of the pagan idols (vss. 15–18). The mention of the thunderstorm recalls the experience of God in nature, but for the most part the psalm expresses the exultation and joy that comes from knowledge of God through the memory of past events.

Psalm 78 gives a long catalogue of events in Israel's history, with the expressed purpose of making known "the glorious deeds of the Lord, his might, and the miracles he has done" (vs. 4). In spirit it is close to Psalm 106, in that it chooses to recall especially the sins of the nation. As in Psalm 106, forgetfulness of the great deeds of God underlies this unlovely story (vss. 11, 42) or "not trusting in the great deeds of God" (vs. 32). Other manifestations of sinfulness are superficial repentance (vss. 34–35), challenging God to provide them with the food they craved (vss. 18–19) and, after entry into the promised land, idolatry and worship at the pagan shrines or "high places" (vs. 58).

There is, however, a special slant to this presentation of the people's history. The psalmist presents these facts, all of which can be documented from other parts of the Scriptures, as a glorification of the southern kingdom and a vilification of the northern. Before the institution of the monarchy, the people of Israel consisted of a loose confederation of tribes, recognizing bonds of kinship and common loyalty to Yahweh. Only from time to time did the tribes undertake concerted action, generally in response to threats from enemies and under the charismatic leadership of such figures as the "saviors of Israel" who are the main heroes of the book of Judges.

Under Saul this loose and informal arrangement was replaced by the monarchy, recognized as a stable institution that would be perpetuated by an agreed-upon line of succession. Already during his reign, Saul's claim to his people's loyalty was challenged by David, of the southern tribe of Judah. After Saul's death, his son Ishbosheth was betrayed by members of his own household (2 Sam. 4:1–12) and David won the allegiance of all the tribes (2 Sam. 5). Under David's successor, Solomon, discontent began to build, and upon Solomon's death in 931 B.C. the natural tendency of the ten northern tribes and the two southern tribes to form two rival groupings reasserted itself. The northern tribes set up a king of their own, Jeroboam I; the south remained loyal, as it always would, to the house of David (1 Kings 11:26–40; 12:1–19). From this time until the fall of the northern kingdom in 722 B.C. to the Assyrians, the chosen race was divided into these two rival kingdoms. The northern kingdom is sometimes called "Israel" (although after the fall of the northern kingdom the word is used to designate the entire chosen race), or "Joseph" or "Ephraim" from the predominant tribal group. The southern kingdom is known as "Judah." Most of the Scriptures are written from the point of view of Judah, which survived the fall of the northern kingdom until Jerusalem itself fell to the Babylonians in 587 B.C. After their return from ensuing exile in 532 B.C. the reconstituted people regarded themselves for all practical purposes as the heirs to the southern kingdom.

The author of Psalm 78 reads history as showing that God favors the southern kingdom and its hero, David. Hence his account of history is not just the recalling of the great deeds of God, but the proclamation of a "law" (vs. 1). The fact that God had abandoned the temple at Shiloh, situated in the territory of the northern kingdom and once the central shrine where the ark of the covenant was preserved (cf. 2 Sam. 6), is for the psalmist evidence that God has withdrawn his favor from the northern tribes (cf. Ps. 78:60–62, 67), and bestowed it on Jerusalem and its king (vss. 68–72). The psalmist's view of the entire history of Israel's sinfulness is colored by this conviction: he consistently claims that the sinfulness of the people is the responsibility of the tribe of Ephraim (vss. 9–10).

Memory is, for the psalmist, a revelation of the way things are, of the laws of reality. His memory, however, is so colored by his present conception of the way things are that it only confirms his convictions. The events he recalls can all be documented from other parts of Scripture, but there is no support there for his belief that the guilty faction was always "Ephraim." His review of the people's history of sinfulness could have been an occasion for deep self-questioning. Instead it becomes an occasion for self-congratulation.

This is typical of the mutual interaction of our belief system and our memory. We build up a story of the way things are from our memory of the past; then our story so colors our remembrance that it is self-perpetuating. Often our "story" will be such as to absolve ourselves of responsibility for our lives and to blame whatever is wrong in them on "others." We need to expose ourselves to our memory with as few preconceptions as possible so that the past may truly speak to us. It will sometimes shatter our preconceived patterns and leave us open to new discovery of the laws of life and the God who is active in our experience.

Psalm 114 shows a great confidence in the power of events to speak for themselves. It simply relives the experience of the parallel miracles at the sea of reeds (Ex. 14–15) and the crossing of the Jordan (Josh. 3). It calls upon the earth to tremble at the coming of God, but for the most part leaves the memory to speak for itself. Psalm 124 is similarly brief. We cannot identify the event it commemorates, but it is a glorious manifestation of God's readiness to save:

> Blessed be Yahweh who did not let us fall
>> a victim to those teeth,
> who let us escape like birds
>> from the fowler's net. (vss. 6–7)

Sometimes thanksgiving prompted by memory can be tempered by the realization that God's work is not yet complete, and the sense of incompleteness leads to prayer of petition. Sometimes the petition is filled with quiet confidence that the great events of the past will be repeated; sometimes it is more anguished, and there is a real concern that the patterns of the past may have changed. Thus in Psalm 106:47 one unresolved event persists in the experience of the psalmist, namely the fact that God's people are scattered among the nations. The confidence that the memory of the past has aroused leads the psalmist to trusting prayer, and once the tension is resolved thanksgiving will be unalloyed:

> Yahweh our God and savior,
> gather us from among the pagans,
> to give thanks to your holy name
> and to find our happiness in thanking you".

There are other psalms, such as 88 and 89, where the psalmist finds it impossible to attain even this stage of completeness about some facet or other of his or her experience. The psalmist is left presenting the broken and incomplete experience to God for completion.

In Psalm 68 a catalogue of God's deeds, not all of which can be identified with certainty, is set in the context of a prayer that God may continue to extend his sway over his enemies (vss. 1–4; 30–35), especially Egypt ("the beast of the reeds" mentioned in vs. 30) and Ethiopia. One does not have the impression that the prayer is prompted by any particularly pressing need; it would sound much more impassioned, for example, if the psalmist were actually threatened by Egyptian aggression. The hope that Egypt and other pagan nations will one day acknowledge Yahweh is part of Israel's vague hopes for the future, and occasionally comes into sharper focus (e.g. Is. 60). In Psalm 68 complacency over God's great deeds predominates over any anxiety about what still remains to be done.

The events recalled in this psalm sound for the most part like a poetic recapitulation of the Exodus and the journey through the desert to the promised land (cf. vss. 7–8; 17–18), which is envisaged in the form of a liturgical procession from Sinai to Mount Zion, where Yahweh takes up his abode in the temple (vss. 24–29). verses 11–16, 22–23 recall some triumph of God over the enemies of his people, but some parts of the description are obscure (notably vss. 13–14), and what we can clearly pick up of the event does not obviously match up with any known event of Israel's history. Bashan, which is mentioned in verses 15 and 22, is a region to the northeast of the Sea of Galilee and has no obvious connection with the events of Exodus, nor do any of the key events of Israel's history occur there. verses 13–14 could suggest that some tribes refused to get involved in a campaign that turned out to be spectacularly successful and profitable for those who took part (a similar incident is described in Judg. 5). It could even be interpreted to mean that no one actually had to get involved in the fighting; all the women had to do was to go out and divide the spoils. The rout of an army by God alone, without human intervention, could, for example, mean that the enemy had to withdraw because of bad weather— and verse 14 does say something about snow on the black mountain. The reference to a dove in verse 13 is still more obscure. Israel is sometimes called God's "dove" (e.g. Ps. 74:19), so perhaps the "dove with burnished wings" is Israel, preening itself on victory won. Or perhaps a bejewelled dove was taken as booty. No exegetically certain answers to these questions can be given, so we are free to picture the scene for ourselves without too much concern for historical exactitude. Whatever it was, the event is for the psalmist a demonstration of God's power to save the downtrodden (vss. 5–6), of that reversal of fortunes whereby the first become last and the last first (vss. 15–16). There are enough instances of this pattern in the Scriptures and in our own personal experience to form the basis of prayer, even if we cannot identify precisely the events spoken of in Psalm 78:11–14.

In the very short Psalm 126, the joyous recall of the return from exile and its feeling of being too good to be true ("when Yahweh brought Zion's captives home, at first it seemed like a dream" vs. 1) prompts the prayer that all those deported may be brought back: "Yahweh, bring all our captives back again like torrents in the Negev" (vs. 4). The return will be like torrents in the Negev (the desolate region to the south of the Dead Sea). Flash floods occur in the desert wadis unexpectedly and tumultuously, seemingly from nowhere, confounding all expectation.

Psalm 132 is imbued with the esteem of David, which gives birth to messianic hope in the Old Testament—the subject of a later chapter. It recalls with esteem David's generous concern for the ark, the throne of God (cf. Ex. 25:22), which, after it had been captured and later restored to the Israelites by the Philistines (cf. 1 Sam. 6), was first left at the house of Obed-edom and later transported to Jerusalem on David's orders (cf. vss. 1–7). On the other hand, God's promises to David are recalled (vss. 11–18). The purpose of this appeal to memory is to plead with God by recalling his promises, and so implicitly appealing to his faithfulness (cf. vss. 8–10).

There are still other psalms where the psalmists find it impossible to attain even that degree of completeness about some facet of their experience that is content with confident petition that God may continue to manifest his saving power. In these psalms, some event has so shattered the psalmists' confidence in the pattern they saw manifested in the past that they now question whether they can confidently expect the pattern to be repeated. Such psalms end with a question mark. The psalmist is left presenting the incompleteness of things to God.

In Psalm 89 the author recalls God's power and majesty manifested and exercised in creation (vss. 9–12), and his generosity manifested in his promises to David (vss. 19–37). The psalmist's own experience, however, seems to belie God's faithfulness, since his promises are not being fulfilled (vss. 38–45). The psalm ends with a plea that God may be swift in fulfilling his promises, since the psalmist feels he has only a short time left in which God can manifest to him his faithfulness since, in line with most Old Testament thought, he presumes that

death is the end of any life worthy of the name: "those who go down
to the pit do not hope in God's faithfulness" (cf. Is. 38:18).

> Remember me, the short times I have left, and the void to which
> you destine humankind. (Ps. 89:47)

The psalm ends, therefore, not just with petition (vss. 47, 50), but with
a number of unresolved questions:

> Yahweh, how much longer will you hide? For ever? How much
> longer must your anger smoulder like a fire? (vs. 46)

> Lord, where are those earlier signs of your love? (vs. 49)

These questions are more than a rhetorically forceful way of expressing petition. They communicate a sense of disorientation, a suspicion
that a former, simpler understanding of the way God deals with his
people will not do any more.

Psalm 44 recalls the mighty deeds that have traditionally formed
the boast and mainstay of Israel's faith (vss. 1–8), but unflinchingly
goes on to record that his present experience does not fit the pattern:

> Yet now you abandon and scorn us,
> you no longer march with our armies,
> you allow the enemy to push us back. . .
> you let us go to the slaughterhouse like sheep. . .
> you sell your own people for next to nothing. . .
> thanks to you, our neighbors insult us. (vss. 9–13)

This experience is all the more bitter in that the psalmist cannot see
any reason for God's changed ways. The prophets traditionally blamed
the people for bringing on themselves the misfortunes that befell them
by their sinful ways. The first known experience of national disaster
that could not conceivably be so explained was the persecution un-
leashed against the Jews in 165 B.C. by the then ruler of Syria, Antiochus IV Epiphanes, who set out forcibly to impose Greek customs on
the Jews. For many at least this could not be accepted without violat-
ing their understanding of God's law, and many chose persecution
rather than accept the new ways. The persecution that broke out could
manifestly not be ascribed to the infidelity of the people; it was the

direct result of their fidelity to the law. The experience was a shock
to the established and simplistic interpretation of suffering as always
and necessarily punishment for evil done, and this shock is reflected
in Psalm 44:

> Had we forgotten the name of our own God,
> and stretched out our hands to another god,
> would not God have found this out,
> he who knows the secrets of the heart?
> No, it is for your sake we are being massacred daily,
> and counted as sheep for the slaughter. (vss. 20–22)

The prayer ends with a desperate appeal to Yahweh's *hesed*.

Psalm 77 is a similar kind of prayer, vibrating with still keener
anguish. The psalmist has "sought the Lord" in his distress (vs. 2) by
turning to the prayer of memory. In fact, it is forced upon him. He
is sleepless and inconsolable, and the memory of the past comes to
him, one has the impression, almost unbidden:

> You stopped me closing my eyes.
> I was too distraught to speak,
> I thought of the olden days,
> years long past came back to me.
> I spent all night murmuring in my heart,
> I pondered and my spirit questioned. (vss. 4–6)

This questioning is very searching. The psalmist faces the possibility
that God's *hesed* has come to an end, that the much-vaunted fidelity
of God is a delusion:

> If the Lord has rejected you, is this final?
> If he withholds his favor, is this forever?
> Is his love over for good,
> and the promise void for all time?
> Has God forgotten to show mercy,
> or has his anger overcome his tenderness?
> This, I said, is what distresses me,
> that the power of the Most High is no longer what it was.
> (vss. 7–10)

In this state of mind he turns to the memory of the past, specifically
of Exodus (vss. 13–20). He imagines God striding through the waters

shrouded in a thunderstorm, which, as we shall see in the following chapter, is frequently regarded as a special manifestation of God. The memory is left hanging in the air; there is no outburst of praise or joy. It is as though the psalmist clings blindly to memory as all he has, though all his disturbing questions remain unanswered. The psalm is an unfinished kind of prayer, prayed in a rather bleak atmosphere. The sense of incompleteness is an honest and adequate reflection of the state of mind from which the prayer comes.

Return to the past enshrined in memory is a basic form of prayer, whether it be consideration of the past for its own sake or prompted by a need to find direction or comfort in a depressing or frightening present. This type of prayer is central also to Christian community prayer, not just because the Christian community continues to use those psalms, which pray from Israel's communial memory, but also because it gives central importance to a specifically Christian form of this prayer in the Eucharist. The Eucharist is essentially a memorial prayer, "proclaiming the Lord's death until he comes" (cf. 1 Cor. 11:27), in response to the Lord's command, "Do this in memory of me" (cf. 1 Cor. 11:25). The Lord's death and resurrection is the central fact of Christian experience, occupying for Christians the central place that the Exodus had held for the Jews. It is far from being an exclusively glorious event; the resurrection does not cancel out the scandal of the cross. Yet the whole mystery is the object of thanksgiving. The very term "eucharist," from the Greek word meaning "thanksgiving," indicates how central the idea of thanksgiving is to the proclamation.

Prayer must above all be "real," dealing with real emotions and not with ersatz, supposedly religious dispositions. Can we, in praying the memory psalms, really feel joy and enthuasiasm and thankfulness for the deeds of God, no matter how impressive, which took place thousands of years ago? Even in Old Testament times this kind of prayer was mainly concerned with the events surrounding the Exodus and they did not, for the most part, continually update these prayers by reference to later events, just as the essentially Christian memorial prayer, the Eucharist, commemorates the one basic event of Christian history, and ignores the nearly two thousand years that have elapsed since.

Both Judaism and Christianity are historical religions. They are based on events that occurred at a certain place and time. But our faith here and now is not primarily an assent to the fact that certain events occurred once and for all in the past, and have receded into the irrecoverable past. They are events that, occurring once and for all in the past, reach down through the ages and touch us here and now. It is of more than antiquarian interest that God brought Israel up out of Egypt. This set a pattern that is repeated again and again throughout history, and its recurrence is a matter of our own personal experience. Anyone who really comes in contact with the God of Israel discovers that he is always and everywhere the God who "brings us up out of the land of Egypt, from the house of slavery" (cf. Ex. 20:2).

The experience of being liberated is not all sweetness and light; it has its frightening, forbidding side, too. It will always involve passing through the sea, "taking the plunge." The sea is destructive, and plunging into it does not look like the way to salvation. Passing through the sea leads out to the desert, which is again an ambiguous reality that exists in the life of everyone. The desert is where one is brought face to face with unadorned reality. It is a place of exhilarating freedom, where the falsity that clutters much of our lives is left behind. The desert has wide horizons. The desert gives an uninterrupted vision of the immensity of the heavens. Yet the human person is never so aware of fragility, of insecurity, and of the uncertainty of his or her very survival, as in the desert. The desert is therefore not so much a geographical location as a state of being. Any person who has lived a lifetime in a city, or in a temperate, well-watered region, can still know the spiritual reality of the desert.

Conquest of the land is also an archetypal sort of experience. It involves finding a niche, a place of rest and security, but coupled with a sort of surprise that this should be the case. Israel never lost a sense that they had not won the enjoyment of the land by their own strength or toil. In a sense, it was never "their" land, as though they possessed it by right of birth. They possessed it as a gift.

Deliverance from exile is in some ways a repetition of the Exodus experience, with one difference. The enslavement experienced in the exile is not a "first time" experience; it has a deadening feel of familiarity about it. Having once experienced deliverance, we find ourselves again enslaved. Deliverance feels all the more distant.

By confining themselves to a simple, basic, almost minimal recitation of the archetypal events of Israel's history, the psalms leave the way open for us to identify with those experiences, rather than overwhelm us with a multitude of historical incidents. The way is open for us to become aware of the enslavement, the risk, the emptiness, the gifted security, and the repetition of the whole pattern again and again in our lives.

The most obvious example among the psalms of this kind of prayer applied to personal rather than to communal experience is Psalm 107. There, different groups who have in various different ways experienced God's saving power are invited to join in thanksgiving and recognition of God's *ḥesed wa'emet*—"his love is everlasting" (vs. 1). The various groups addressed are those who have been rescued from captivity in foreign lands (vss. 2–3), who have escaped after being lost in the desert (vss. 4–7), who have been imprisoned for their misdeeds and are now freed (vss. 10–14), who have suffered sickness and are now cured (vss. 17–20), or who have been close to shipwreck (vss. 23–30). The psalm concludes with a general consideration of God's power to bring down the mighty and exalt the lowly (vss. 33–42). Considering these facts leads to wisdom and knowledge of Yahweh:

> If you are wise study these things,
> and realize how Yahweh shows his love. (vs. 43)

Literally to have experienced even one of the vicissitudes mentioned, apart from sickness, would be, in our modern society, rather rare. However, they do lend themselves to a kind of metaphorical application to a host of personal experiences. It is also striking that most of them match up with the archetypal events of Israel's history: enslavement and deliverance, the desert, and the threatening destructiveness of the sea.

Most of us are familiar with the feeling that our personal freedom is being unjustly restricted, perhaps that we are prevented from being our true selves, by the expectations that others impose on us; we are captives in a strange land (vss. 2–3). The experience of having lost one's way in life and being isolated from one's fellows, who give the impression of being at ease and knowing the way, is far from uncommon:

> Some lost their way in the wilds and the desert,
> not knowing how to reach an inhabited town. (vs. 4)

At other times we experience being hemmed in and restricted in our freedom, but we can no longer throw the responsibility for this on others. We are not being held captive, but we must accept the responsibility for our state, even if we can no longer find the way out:

> Living in gloom and darkness, fettered in misery
> and irons,
> for defying the orders of God,
> for scorning the advice of the Most High. (vss. 10–11)

Similarly, the description of imminent shipwreck readily evokes our experience of other kinds of storms, of a world out of control, perhaps especially of those frightening emotional storms that can blow apparently out of nowhere and threaten our competence to live and cope:

> Flung to the sky, then plunged to the depths,
> they lost their nerve in the ordeal,
> staggering and reeling like drunkards,
> with all their seamanship adrift. (vss. 26–27)

There are many psalms that provide us with paradigms of prayer in threatening circumstances. Psalm 107 invites us to incorporate the past experience of such vicissitudes into our consciously assimilated personal histories. We are invited not to take it for granted that we have survived threats to our physical or psychical well-being, but to savor and appreciate the fact that we have weathered the storms.

While Psalm 107 invites us to scrutinize our past and let what emerges emerge, letting the situations described evoke our memories, most of the other psalms that draw on private memory are not so open-ended; they either take the form of joyfully and thankfully reliving a particular experience of God's saving power, or they return to the past with a view to discovering the direction or courage to face a present disaster.

Psalm 30 is an example of the former type of prayer. In it the psalmist relives his experience of falling from a state of security and even smugness ("in my prosperity I used to say 'Nothing can ever shake me!' " vs. 6) to terror ("then you hid your face and I was terrified" vs. 7). So deeply does he become immersed in the memory that he prays again with all the terror of that time of God's absence:

Yahweh, I call to you
I beg my God to pity me.
What do you gain by my blood if I go to the Pit?
Can the dust praise you or proclaim your faithfulness?"
(vs. 9)

He has, however, already experienced salvation. Already in verses 1–3 he proclaimed his experience of God's saving power: "You have helped me up, and not let my enemies gloat over me . . . you have healed me . . . you have brought my life up from Sheol . . . you revived me." He returns to this exultant proclamation in verses 11–12. The most obvious interpretation of his suffering is that he was ill: "to go down to the pit" is a Hebrew way of saying "to die." However, it can easily serve as a metaphorical description of other forms of intense suffering.

Psalm 22 is an example of the second kind of appeal to the past. The dominating experience out of which the psalm is prayed is of desolation and suffering:

My God, my God, why have you deserted me?
How far from saving me, the words I groan.
I call all day, my God, but you never answer,
all night long I call, and cannot rest. (vss. 1–2)

Present distress recalls by contrast past joy and the experience of God's nearness, both in the common memory of the whole people, and in the psalmist's private store of memories:

Yet, Holy One,
You who make your home in the praises of Israel,
in you our fathers put their trust,
they trusted and you rescued them;
they called to you for help and they were saved,
they never trusted in vain. . . . (vss. 3–5)

And, after once again immersing himself in his present misery (vss. 6–8):

Yet you drew me out of the womb,
you entrusted me to my mother's breasts;
placed in your lap from my birth,
from my mother's womb you have been my God. (vss. 9–10)

This to-and-fro movement from present distress to memory of past experience of God does not of itself, in Psalm 22, resolve the present crisis. Resolution comes (vss. 22–31) after the psalmist has recognized that he himself is incapable of solving his present predicament and acknowledges his impotence by turning to God in petition:

> Do not stand aside, trouble is near,
> I have no one to help me! (vs. 11; cf. vss. 19–21)

Later we shall look to Psalm 22 and the many similar psalms to discern a model of prayer in desolation or distress. Here we simply note that memory plays a part in human coping with distress and therefore has a part in that pouring out of the heart before God which is prayer. Memory always contributes something to our present experience; about this we have no choice. We face the present with the baggage we have collected throughout our journey through life. It can be a liability, but it will not be discarded. We can flee from the present into our memories and attempt to live in the past, to our own loss. We can leave our memories unexamined and they will continue to influence, and perhaps warp, our perceptions of the present. We can, however, enter into our memories and hold them up to the light so that they may themselves be enlightened.

What I have called prayer from memory involves, in its basic form, going back, with God, into memory with as open an attitude as we are capable of, to let the past speak to us—and to let what will emerge emerge. It is basic to biblical faith to be confident that the process will ultimately reveal to us a God of *hesed wa'emet*, of generosity and faithfulness. One can also resort to memory in search of something quite specific. Having once had the experience of the past revealing to us a God passionately concerned for us and our welfare, we can feel the need or be impelled to get in touch with this experience in times of distress when our hold on this conviction becomes tenuous. The psalms so far considered in any detail are prayers where recourse to memory is of special importance; there will be many other psalms where it plays a more incidental role.

5 ⚜

Prayer from Awe

Just as reviewing the past in memory can convey a sense of God as an active force in our lives, so the experience of the material world around us can give us another intuition of divinity. I am not speaking here of logically constructed "proofs" of God's existence, which argue from the existence of finite beings to the necessity of an infinite cause; this is a dauntingly abstract undertaking. One may be unable logically to refute an argument of this kind, and still feel dissatisfied or inclined to ask "So what?" At their best, such arguments encapsulate in logical form much more elemental intuitions about the nature of reality and the ultimate ground of all being. They may even have the effect of so dessicating an experience of the divine as to create problems rather than clarify, just as the surgeon's scalpel can sometimes destroy life, and what is left on the operating table is a pale, lifeless shadow of the being the scalpel laid open.

Rather we are dealing with a prayerful savoring of that experience that is not denied even to atheists—the sense of being suddenly struck by an almost painful awareness of the beauty and grandeur of creation, to which we respond with awe.

Something of the complex experience of awe is expressed in the description of Moses' encounter with God in the burning bush, in Exodus 3:1–6. Moses' first reaction is to draw near and see more: " 'I must go and look at this strange sight,' he said, 'and see why the bush is not burned' " (vs. 3). No sooner is this desire conceived, however, than he knows that it is never to be fulfilled; he is somehow attracted and repelled at once:

> "Moses, Moses!" he said. "Here I am," he answered. "Come no
> nearer," he said; "Take off your shoes, for the place on which you
> stand is holy ground" (vss. 4–5).

Awe is compounded of admiration, fascination, and a certain fear.
The divine quality that arouses this response is expressed in the word
"holiness," which expresses, not primarily the idea of moral perfection, but the idea of "otherness," "transcendence." God is at once
supremely desirable yet unattainable. The discovery of God is at once
satisfying and frustrating.

This sense of awe, of being transcended, of discovering a power and
a beauty that so far exceed anything we can do or be, is an almost
universal human experience. Human beings have for the most part
responded rather unreflectingly by concluding that the things that
have impressed them are somehow divine or the abode of divine
beings. Jacob's recognition of the "holiness" of Bethel, described in
Genesis 28:10–22 is typical of this sort of experience, and his words
have been echoed in human minds and hearts throughout history:

> How awe-inspiring this place is! This is nothing less than the
> house of God; this is the gate of heaven! (vs. 17).

Poets and artists are more attuned to this kind of intuition than the
ordinary person, but few people are utterly devoid of a sense of the
mysterious dimension of the world around them, even if they have
trained themselves to discount or ignore it.

The experience can be interpreted in many ways. Modern Western
man, for whom the universe has been radically "de-mythologized"
and reduced to a collection of interacting forces, will perhaps be
inclined to stop short at the experience and ask no further questions.
Polytheist and animist cultures assume that there is a personal, superhuman, divine or semi-divine being revealed in each of these experiences, and so arrive at a picture of a universe peopled by myriads of
superhuman beings. The Old Testament generally does not quarrel
with the belief that there are many superhuman beings present and
active in the universe. In fact, until medieval times Christian theology
ascribed the movements of the stars in the heavens to angels. But any
experience of what is good or great or beautiful is seen as a revelation
of a transcendent goodness that is not to be identified with any of the
lesser realities which embody something of it.

The poet Wordsworth regarded anyone who remained unmoved by the sight of London at early morning as "dull of soul." Wisdom 13 regards the person who does not have this intuition of transcendent goodness as "naturally stupid":

> Yes, naturally stupid are all who have not known God,
> and who, from the good things that are seen,
> have not been able to discover Him who is,
> or, by studying the works, have failed to recognize
> the Artificer. (vss. 1–2)

Wisdom 13 can even claim to understand the person who is so bedazzled by the beauties of the heavens as to identify the stars or natural forces to be themselves gods:

> If, charmed by their beauty, they have taken things for gods,
> let them know how much the Lord of these excels them,
> since the very Author of beauty created them. . . .
> small blame, however, attaches to these men,
> for perhaps they only go astray
> in their search for God and their eagerness to find him.
> Living among his works, they strive to comprehend them
> and fall victim to appearances, seeing so much beauty.
> (vss. 3.6–7)

The author cannot however, find it in himself to sympathize with those who consider that man-made idols are gods (a position that few, if any, "idolaters" actually take; even the most naive have some sense that an artifact represents a bigger reality).

The poets who expressed in the psalms their sense of God present and active in creation had a picture of the universe that is far removed from our own, though perhaps close to some of the immediate *impressions* we cannot help but experience. They presumed that the earth was flat and, though we know better, we cannot avoid the impression that—even to the astronomer—it *looks* flat. The psalmists thought that this flat earth was covered with a crystal dome—and the sky still looks dome-shaped to us. They called this dome the "firmament" (*raqi^{ac}*). Underneath the earth, and above the firmament, the Hebrews imagined a boundless, uncontrollable and potentially destructive sea of water. This conception, so strange to us, was supported by observation: the waters above the firmament sometimes seeped through in the form of rain, and the waters below the earth could be reached by digging wells. At certain points there was a gap in the earth, and the waters showed through in the form of seas, lakes, and rivers. The waters were destructive, unfriendly to man, and only the power of God kept them at bay (cf. Ps. 104:8–9). Man's survival in the face of these destructive forces was a constant source of amazement.

Although it is hard for us to feel that we live surrounded by water, we can at least identify with the Hebrew sense of human fragility. Our sophisticated understanding of the delicate balance of factors that are involved in human survival, and of the immense cosmic forces to which we are subject, can convey to us some of the sense of human fragility that the Hebrews experienced at the thought of the waters surrounding their world. The earth was supposed to be supported in the waters by pillars, though no one could claim to know what supported the pillars themselves (cf. Job. 38:6). Maybe we can find a baffling modern equivalent to the enigma of the pillars if we ask ourselves "Where is the universe?", "What exists outside of space?", or "What happens when we reach the end of the universe?"

More often, however, the experience recorded in the nature psalms is not bound to any one way of picturing the universe. We do not have to share the Hebrew belief that the stars were lights attached to the inside of the dome of the firmament in order to share the awe that the sight of the night sky inspires in the author of Psalm 8. Here the poet expresses the sense of human littleness in the face of the universe that we still experience if we find ourselves out under the stars:

> I look at the heavens, made by your fingers,
> at the moon and the stars you set in place . . .
> Ah, what is man that you should spare
> a thought for him,
> the son of man that you should care for him?
> (vss. 3–4)

The humility that is impressed on us in these circumstances is not crushing, and does not leave us demoralized. As always, a God-given experience cannot prove ultimately destructive of human dignity or a true sense of self-worth. So the psalmist proceeds from the sense of littleness and insignificance to a sense of his dignity:

Yet you made him little less than a god,
you have crowned him with glory and splendor,
made him lord over the work of your hands,
set all things under his feet. . . ." (vss. 5–6)

Psalm 8 therefore celebrates the paradox of the human person, insignificant and aware of this insignificance, yet, deep down, bold enough to claim to be "almost divine." Exulting in the mystery of human existence, we are moved to admire God who is the ultimate ground of the paradox. "Yahweh, our Lord, how great is your name through all the earth" is the antiphonal refrain that opens and closes the psalm (vss. 1, 9).

Psalm 19 is partly a psalm exulting in the law of God, a type of prayer we shall consider more fully later. But in verses 1–6 the psalmist is immersed in the glories of nature, which for him reveal the majesty of God. The experience of the day reveals certain aspects of God's glory, and is repeated day after day. Night reveals another aspect of the mystery, and is repeated again and again. Hence "Day discourses (of the glory of God) to day, night to night hands on the knowledge" (vs. 2). The message is clear, yet not articulated in ordinary human words. (vss. 3–4). Above all the psalmist, like millions of human beings before and after him—from the sun-worshipers of various cultures to the "sun-worshipers" who throng modern beaches—exults in the wonder of the sun, which he sees as a giant running a daily course across the heavens and mysteriously returning to its starting point for the new day (vss. 5–6). This is an impression that we, with all our astronomical sophistication, cannot avoid.

The 29th Psalm celebrates another manifestation of God in nature: the thunderstorm. Frequently the approach of God is described in the psalms and elsewhere in the Old Testament as accompanied by the clouds, thunder, lightning, and downpour of rain that occur in a thunderstorm. Obviously one feels awe in the presence of such occurrences and thus through them experience a sense of the divine.

Psalm 29 is also an example of a technique not frequently used in the psalms, but characteristic of early forms of Middle-Eastern poetry. Hebrew poetry normally employs the device known as parallelism. Usually this means that everything is expressed twice, in parallel form. However, the earliest forms of this device were not satisfied to have the content of each statement expressed at least twice. In its earliest form the technique tends to repeat not only the content, but the actual phraseology, so that successive lines all but repeat initial statements word for word, advancing only by minimal additions to or variations of the original statement.

Thus the first lines of Psalm 29 play with the expression "Pay tribute to Yahweh" and with the word "glory":

> *Pay tribute to Yahweh*, you sons of God,
> *pay tribute to Yahweh* of *glory* and power,
> *pay tribute to Yahweh* of the *glory* of his name. (vss. 1–2)

The focus then shifts to another phrase: the "voice of Yahweh" (which means the thunder):

> *The voice of Yahweh* over the waters,
>   Yahweh over the multitudinous waters,
> *The voice of Yahweh* in power,
> *The voice of Yahweh* in splendor,
> *The voice of Yahweh* shatters the cedars . . .
> *The voice of Yahweh* sharpens lightning shafts,
> *The voice of Yahweh* sets the wilderness shaking . . .
> *The voice of Yahweh* sets the terebinths shuddering.
>   (vss. 3–5, 7–9)

Finally, "sits enthroned" becomes the key phrase in vss. 9–10:

> Yahweh *sat enthroned* for the flood,
> Yahweh *sits enthroned* as king forever. (vss. 9–10)

The effect of this very repetitious technique can be quite overpowering, hammering home an idea and a sound with pounding insistency, which, in this case, recalls the relentless repetition of the thunderclaps that are the "voice of God." The image of God presiding, enthroned, over the waters is based, first, on the Hebrew conception of the universe, which locates heaven somewhere above the upper waters (cf. Ps. 104:2). But it expresses something more than a mere locality. It expresses something of God's serene command over the chaotic and destructive power of the waters, which seem to have broken loose in a thunderstorm, but in fact are subject and obedient to the voice of God booming in the thunder. Psalm 29 goes some way toward re-creating the experience of a thunderstorm and inviting us to discover God in it.

Psalm 93 is similar in thought, and makes some use of the highly repetitious technique employed in Psalm 29. However, it is not as graphic as the latter, and the serenity of God is triumphant through-out—despite the mutter of rebellion in the third verse:

> Yahweh, the rivers raise,
> the rivers raise their voice,
> the rivers raise their thunders.

But this is rather like the mutter of thunder in the distance—sullen, but no real threat. The full forces of chaos never break out:

> Greater than the voice of mighty waters,
> transcending the waves of the sea,
> Yahweh reigns on high. (vs. 4)

The 104th Psalm celebrates creation from quite a different view-point. The psalms so far considered in this chapter have described the experience of the awe-inspiring majesty of nature, and in Psalm 29 the rather frightening experience of creation seemingly out of control. But Psalm 104 expresses a rather cheerful sense of the orderliness of a creation in which the psalmist feels very much at home. One is not forced to choose between these two ways of experiencing man's rela-tionship with the world around him. Both are real, though partial, expressions of the alternatives.

Verses 2–12 in Psalm 104 describe the process of creation. God stretches out the heavens—the firmament—and takes up his abode above the waters. The whole process is a work of the spirit or wind (cf. Gen. 1:2). The earth is fixed, and the waters confined to their allotted place. Although there is an inevitable reference to the threat that the waters pose to the stability of the earth (vs. 9), the comforting awareness of God's control of them is stronger than any unease at the thought.

Verses 13–20 describe the disposition of the world once it has been constituted. The overriding sense is one of order—"a place for every-thing and everything in its place." All the needs of man and beast alike are provided for. God provides rain and water from springs, reducing the ungovernable expanse of the "waters" to manageable proportions so that what would, uncontrolled, overwhelm and destroy both man and beast, becomes their servant. God provides light and darkness (the Hebrews were inclined to see darkness as something just as real as light), and the author sees a purpose in darkness: it is the time allotted to the wild animals, just as day is allotted to human activity. The ocean itself begins to look friendly through the optimistic eyes of this psalmist. Even Leviathan, the great sea monster who is usually envisaged as a personification of the sea, with all the nastiness and destructiveness of the sea itself, is here seen as a creature of God, made in a moment of God's playfulness. Perhaps the psalmist would be inclined to see something incongruous and wildly funny in the darker forces of nature—a joke played on us by God which we have not yet fully appreciated!

Even the cycle of life-suffering-death-new life, all of which is established by God and involves his giving or withdrawing the gift of breath or the spirit (vss. 27–29) is seen rather as a positive process by which God continually renews the world (vs. 30).

We do not always resonate to Psalm 104 and its relentlessly optimistic view of the world. Sometimes we are very aware of demonic forces at work, or we are oppressed by the cycle of death and rebirth. There is a time for that and a form of prayer suitable for such times. But Psalm 104 is for the cheerful times, the sunny spring days when we exult in the prodigality of nature, or the times when, simply because of our own sense of inner well-being, we feel reconciled with the created universe:

> You are a child of the universe.
> No less than the rocks and the trees,
> you have a right to be here. ("Desiderata")

Psalm 139 also is a celebration of God as known in creation, but instead of turning outward, the psalmist turns attention on himself. Just as an appreciation of the surrounding world can lead the believer to discover and praise God, so an appreciation of oneself can do likewise. The psalmist is aware of himself encompassed by God and his breath. It is not an oppressive awareness, though it is possible to feel the closeness of God as oppressive, and it is quite proper to express this in prayer, as is done in the 39th Psalm. Psalm 139, however, is prayed out of one of those integrating and health-giving moments when one is happy to be oneself.

The psalmist is aware of the limits of his own self-understanding, but basks in the sense of being known exhaustively by God:

> It was you who created my inmost self,
> who put me together in my mother's womb.
> For all these mysteries I thank you,
> for the wonder of myself,
> for the wonder of your works.
> You know me through and through,
> from having watched my bones take shape,
> when I was being formed in secret,
> knitted together in the limbo of the womb. (vss. 11–14)

Two psalms, 65 and 67, are songs of thanksgiving for the harvest. This is not so profound or mystical an experience as the intuition of God revealed in the beauty of nature. It may be rather difficult for people living in an urban and prosperous environment, cushioned from the impact of the vagaries of nature, to appreciate the joy of a good year in an agricultural community with a subsistence economy. The farmer is at the mercy of the elements, which will mean success or failure of his year's efforts, and, in a subsistence economy, can mean the difference between life and death. Conversely, his joy at a good season will be correspondingly greater. Perhaps we can best empathize with the sentiments expressed in these psalms by recalling times when our projects have turned out successful only after we have invested much personal effort, where our well-being hung on the outcome, and we knew that success depended upon factors outside our control.

Both Psalms 65 and 67 imagine the gentiles noting and reacting to the special favor that God has shown Israel in providing a bountiful harvest. In Psalm 65:8 those who live at "the portals of morning and evening" (that is, the gates through which the sun rises and sets, therefore at the easternmost and westernmost points on a flat earth) are thrown into panic at the coming of Yahweh, but Psalm 67 takes a kinder view and has the nations join in the rejoicing of God's people.

A sense of the divine can be conveyed by material things because they incorporate and manifest something of transcendent beauty. Yet constantly throughout the experience of mankind there have been "holy places" where people flock because, by common consent, they recognize the presence of the divine. In such instances, an interplay of influences all help to introduce devotees to their own personal discovery of the holiness of the place. Very often the place itself impresses, either by natural beauty or by human adornment. Yet the associations it holds, the very reputation it has for being a place where God is present, all contribute to predispose the pilgrim to discover that God is there. If modern pilgrims are moved by visiting Jerusalem it is not just because of the appeal of its narrow streets or exotic architecture or the beauty of its setting. The fact that events of crucial significance to our faith took place there is important, but so is the knowledge that for millennia people have recognized Jerusalem as a holy city. Yet would historic associations alone be enough if the ancient buildings were all razed and replaced by glass and steel skyscrapers?

Similarly, I believe that the faith of the ancient Israelites in the holiness of Jerusalem was not based simply on a blind acceptance of Exodus 25:22, which promises that the ark of the covenant is the place where God will be present. In fact, had people not experienced for themselves the reality of God's presence in the temple and in Jerusalem, the claim that he had promised to be present there could hardly have been accepted as truly the Word of God. Belief does not grow out of creeds; creeds grow out of belief.

A number of psalms express the psalmists' experience of Jerusalem and the temple as the place of God's presence. Psalm 48 exults in the beauty of the city:

> Yahweh is great and supremely to be praised
>   in the city of our God.
> The holy mountain, beautiful where it rises,
> joy of the whole world. (vss. 1–2)

Later we find a loving appreciation of the city's strength and beauty:

> Go through Zion, walk round her,
>   counting her towers,
> admiring her walls, reviewing her palaces. (vss. 12–13)

Psalm 125 exults in the sense of security and impregnability that the psalmist experiences there, and which leads him into a sense of God's protection:

> Those who trust in Yahweh are like Mount Zion,
> unshakeable, standing forever.
> Jerusalem! Encircled by mountains,
> so Yahweh encircles his people,
> now and for always! (vss. 1–2)

Delight in the temple and in God are closely intertwined in Psalm 84:

> How I love your palace, Yahweh Sabaoth!
> How my soul yearns and pines for Yahweh's courts!
> (vss. 1–2a)

This is followed immediately by:

> My heart and my flesh sing for joy
> to the living God. (vs. 2b)

The poet envies those who can remain constantly in the house of God, the sparrows and the temple personnel (vss. 3–4), but he himself rejoices in the prospect of making pilgrimage to Jerusalem (vss. 5–7). Esteem for the house of David is naturally bound up with attachment to Jerusalem, the city of David, and the psalmist's prayer for himself and his companions spills over to prayer for the king, the "anointed one" ("Messiah"). The messianic ideal and ethos in the psalms will be considered in more detail later.

Other psalms exult in the sense of national unity that the poet experiences at Jerusalem. Thus Psalm 122:

> Here the tribes come up, the tribes of Yahweh.
> They come to praise Yahweh's name
> as he ordered Israel,
> Here where the tribunals of justice are,
> the royal tribunals of David. (vss. 3–5)

Psalm 133 also celebrates the sense of brotherly love that is experienced especially in Jerusalem, "copious as Hermon dew falling on the heights of Zion, where Yahweh confers his blessing, life forever" (vs. 3).

In Psalm 87 the poet looks forward to the time when the unity experienced and hymned in Psalms 122 and 133 will break through its national limitations, and the feeling that he has for the city of Jerusalem will be shared by all nations, especially those whose relationship with the chosen race has been most unhappy: Egypt, Babylonia, Philistia, Tyre, and Ethiopia.

Psalm 46 expresses a confidence in God's care for Jerusalem in the refrain

> Yahweh Sabaoth is on our side,
> our citadel, the God of Jacob! (vss. 3, 7, 11)

Verses 5–6 may refer to the mysterious deliverance of the city from the siege of Sennacherib, described in Isaiah 36–37, or perhaps they are a general summary of the experience of God's special protection of the city. This faith in Jerusalem's impregnability suffered a blow with the fall of Jerusalem to the Babylonians in 587 B.C., yet survived in some less crass form.

The spring of Siloam also gives the psalmist a sense of the unfailing power of God to save:

> There is a river whose streams refresh the city of God,
> and it sanctifies the dwelling of the most High,
> God is inside the city, she can never fall. (vss. 4–5)

The spring is the only source of fresh running water for the city, located at the foot of the slope on which the city was built, outside the city walls. To ensure an unfailing supply of fresh water within the walls in case of siege, a tunnel had been cut back into the slope, carrying the waters of the spring back under the walls to a shaft sunk within the walls, the original access to the spring being then obstructed with stones. It was an impressive feat of primitive engineering, and probably prompted in the psalmist something of the respect for and delight in human achievement that we feel today when confronted by a marvel of modern engineering. The spring itself is an amazingly copious source of fresh water flowing, seemingly, from nowhere in the rock. Like God's help, it is abundant and unfailing, but unnerving in that one has no visible assurance that it will continue to flow.

These psalms express a true religious experience of God present in the temple. Yet this kind of spirituality has its limitations and pitfalls. It can degenerate into an almost superstitious obsession with a place, into a concern for externals which can be stultifying. Formalistic participation in ritual can become a substitute for real meeting with God. From earliest times the prophets protested against abuses of the mystique of the temple. Jesus looked forward to the time when localized worship would be transcended and "true worshippers will worship the Father in spirit and truth" (Jn. 4:21–24). At his trial he was accused of a subversive attitude toward the temple: "We heard him say, 'I am going to destroy this Temple made by human hands, and in three days build another, not made by human hands. . .' " (Mk. 24:58). Stephen, the first Christian martyr, was also accused of speaking "against the holy place and the law" (Acts 6:15).

One New Testament way of adapting Old Testament texts about the temple is simply to apply them all to Christ himself. He is now the new temple, the place where man meets God and God makes himself available to man. For the Christian, "Jerusalem" becomes a hope, a heavenly reality barely glimpsed. In Revelation 21–22 the author describes a heavenly future Jerusalem that will be God's gift to man, and which will have no temple, "since the Lord God Almighty and the Lamb were themselves the Temple" (Rev. 21:22). In Galatians 4:25–26 Paul contrasts the present Jerusalem, an earthly city, with the "free" Jerusalem which is "above." The ecstatic descriptions of the beauties of Jerusalem found in the psalms thus become a way of picturing that hoped-for state where God will be all in all.

This is the classical Christian adaptation of the Jewish feeling for the temple and for Jerusalem. There is perhaps also a simpler, more direct way in which we can identify in ourselves sentiments like those expressed in the psalms exulting the Holy City. Many people have in their experience one or more personal "holy places," which by reason of a combination of factors such as beauty, historical associations, personal experiences of God, or a combination of all these, have become places where we meet God. Such experiences have a beneficent and salvific effect in our lives, and can be profitably relived and prayerfully savored, just as the pious Jew, in the psalms just considered, relived and savored his experience of God linked with Jerusalem and the temple.

6 ⚜

Exulting in God

So far I have stressed contemplation of the works of God, either in history (prayer from memory), or in creation (the psalms that I call prayer from awe). Such contemplation leads, by its nature, to joy, thanksgiving, exultation in God. There are many psalms that express this exultation in God but devote very little, if any, attention to the contemplation of God in his works, which is the ultimate ground for exultation. At first this may seem a rather fine line to draw, since one cannot speak of the God of Israel and his attributes without some implicit reference to his deeds. But, psychologically, to contemplate the past or the created reality and let them speak to us of God is not at all the same as exulting in the attributes of God, already known and acknowledged.

The patterns of God's action

Perhaps the best example of the latter kind of prayer is Psalm 117, which is nothing more than an expression of joy in God's generosity and fidelity (*ḥesed wa'emet*). Without a background of experience of God's dealings with his people and with individuals this would be empty and meaningless, a mere formula. Prayer of this kind, consisting as it does of recall of the "attributes" of God, needs to be constantly revitalized by a return to the experience of God as described in the previous two chapters—if it is not to become unreal, an exercise in juggling words or concepts, drifting away from contact with reality.

Psalm 145 illustrates how the proclamation of God's attributes rests on the prayer of memory. The psalmist knows that to praise God and "bless his name" (vs. 1), and to measure his greatness (vs. 2), one must tell the story of his deeds:

Celebrating your acts of power,
one age shall praise your doings to another.
Oh, the splendor of your glory, your renown,
I tell myself the story of your marvelous deeds!
                                        (vss. 4–5)

The psalmist does not, however, explicitly recall events, but rather enumerates the qualities of God that are evident in the constantly repeated pattern of his deeds: fearsome power (vs. 6), goodness and justice (vs. 7), kindness and compassion, long-suffering and generosity (vs. 8—all qualities proclaimed in Exodus 34:6), and faithfulness (vs. 13). It is as though these abstractions are a shorthand way of recalling a multitude of events.

This psalm is also the first example we have seen of an alphabetical psalm. Each line of the original version begins with the succeeding letter of the Hebrew alphabet. The psalmists occasionally subjected themselves to this requirement as an exercise in virtuosity, just as a poet in English may choose to subject himself to the rigorous forms and rhyming patterns of the ode or the sonnet.

Psalm 33 is a hymn of praise of God's word, which, in the Old Testament, is typically thought of as a commanding rather than a revealing word. Some human beings possess the gift of authority that gives their word special power; one tends instinctively to take notice and obey. God's word possesses this quality of power: he calls things into being by his word of command (vss. 6–9) and intervenes in history in the same way (vss 10–19), thwarting the designs of the nations (assumed to be, of course, opposed to God and his ways), and defending the defenseless. The qualities of God's word that arouse the psalmist's enthusiasm are its power and reliability ("faithfulness").

He spoke, and it was created;
he commanded, and there it stood" (vs. 9).
"The word of Yahweh is integrity itself,
all he does is done faithfully. . . . (vs. 4)

The Christian recalls the theology of Jesus as the Word of God, active in creation and intervening in history to do God's will, especially as this is expressed in John 1:1–18.

Exulting in God also involves trust in him, verbalized toward the end of the psalm:

> Our throat (*nephesh*) waits on Yahweh,
> he is our help and shield,
> our hearts rejoice in him,
> we trust in his holy name. . . . (vss. 20–21)

Conversely, any other source of confidence is illusory and therefore a temptation:

> A king is not saved by his great army;
> a warrior is not delivered by his great strength.
> The war horse is a vain hope for victory,
> and by its great might it cannot save. (vss. 16–17)

Psalm 113 praises God's greatness, but above all his concern for the downtrodden and despised:

> He raises the poor from the dust;
> he lifts the needy from the dunghill
> to give them a place with princes,
> with the princes of his people.
> He enthrones the barren woman in her house
> by making her the happy mother of children. (vss. 6–9)

Psalm 98 may be an act of thanksgiving for some particular benefit, though it is not described in detail; God's *hesed wa'emet* are manifested in whatever the event was. Psalm 100 praises the basic divine qualities of "generosity and faithfulness" (*hesed we'emuna* rather than the more usual *hesed wa'emet; 'emuna* comes from the same root as *'emet* and has the same sense.

Psalm 47 celebrates God's giving victory to Israel in battle. Since it recalls also the gift of the land ("our heritage," vs. 4) the victory would be particularly the conquest of the nations who originally inhabited the land of Palestine:

> He brings peoples under our dominion
> he puts nations under our feet;
> for us he chooses our heritage—
> the pride of Jacob, whom he loved. (vss. 3–4)

Psalm 76 also celebrates the God-given dominion over other nations that the chosen race enjoys. Attempted rebellion or resistance to God's dominion only adds to his glory:

> Man's wrath only adds to your glory,
> the survivors of your wrath you bind around you like a
> girdle. (vs. 10)

Psalms 145 through 150 are a series whose theme is praise. They repeat the themes contained in the preceding psalms we have considered, and ensure that the entire collection of psalms ends on a note of exultation. Psalm 146 contrasts the power of God with the puniness of princes (vs. 2), and exults that his power is at the service of the downtrodden and defenseless (vss. 7–9). Psalm 147 repeats these themes: God is on the side of the downtrodden (vss. 1–9) and is not overawed by creatures' power (vss. 10–11). Verses 12–20 celebrate the power of God's word, manifested in his control of the elements (vss. 15–18), and in the law communicated to his chosen people (vss. 19–20), which the psalmist ranks among their special privileges. Psalm 148 calls on brute creation to praise God, whose lordship it recognizes by doing his will (vss. 1–10), then turns to the human race for praise (vss. 11–14).

Psalm 149 exults in the strength that God grants his people, and the fact the he delights in them (vs. 4). It takes up still more strongly a theme in Psalms 47 and 76, namely, that God's people share in his lordship, wreaking his vengeance on his enemies. This is an image of great poetic force:

> Let the high praises of God be in their throats,
> and two-edged swords in their hands,
> to wreak vengeance on the nations
> and chastisement of the peoples,
> to bind their kings in chains,
> and their nobles in fetters of iron,
> to execute on them the judgment that is decreed.
> This is the glory of all his faithful ones. (vss. 5–9)

To exult in God-given victory, as do Psalms 47 and 76, already causes some qualms. To look forward to inflicting divine punishment on one's enemies, as does Psalm 149, is worse still. We can interpret such images metaphorically: "Our enemies" are all that stand in the way of our enjoying fully the life that God wills for us. Ultimately, then, our truest enemies are within. They can be vanquished only by God's power. We can legitimately rejoice in such victory over them as has already been ours, and look forward to extending this victory further.

However, if we let our imagination play freely on the images suggested in these warlike psalms, and resist the temptation to censor it quickly and divert it into the channels we have already decided are acceptable, we may find that these psalms reveal some surprising things about our own hearts. The urge to dominate or be revenged on those who disagree with us is not dead, although we may have become sophisticated enough not to let the urge express itself in gross ways. The warlike psalms may awaken some unexpected echoes in our hearts. And if they do reveal unexpected violence in our hearts, this is not just an occasion for suppressing it more effectively. If we are genuinely stirred to indignation by some way or other of acting, by some person or group of people, this reveals to us where our hearts are. We are by nature inclined to fight for what we passionately believe in. Any person of conviction has an inner fire that demands constructive expression.

Conversely, if we can honestly feel no empathy with the violent emotions expressed in these psalms, if we even feel a positive repugnance or embarrassment about them, we cannot immediately congratulate ourselves on being an enlightened or tolerant person. Apathy or fear of getting involved can masquerade under the guise of tolerance. If we do not have even the potential to be destructive, we can seriously ask ourselves whether we are capable of constructive action either, or whether we are in fact so destructive in our attitudes that we will not allow ourselves to tolerate the possibility of our own destructiveness.

Psalm 150 provides a conclusion to the collection of psalms, calling on all the instruments of a biblical orchestra to join in the praises of God.

Psalm 95 hails God as "rock" (vs. 1) and as "shepherd" (vs. 7). The former image suggests solidity, reliability, support. It is a concrete way of expressing the abstract idea that God is the ground of our being and activity. It is perhaps not by accident that his "rocklike" qualities are manifested in his command of creation (vss. 3–5). He proves himself a shepherd by his care of his people (vs. 7).

The psalmist rejoices that Yahweh is Lord of other gods. (vs. 3). It is usual in the Old Testament that the existence of other gods be taken for granted, although they pose no threat to Yahweh's lordship. Sometimes they are imagined as forming part of his heavenly court (cf. Ps. 82:1). Deuteronomy 4:15–20 goes so far as to suggest that the gods of pagan nations have been so designated by Yahweh himself. It is only after the exile (mid-sixth century B.C.) that a tendency emerges to ridicule the gods of other nations as being nothing more than the images that represent them, as in Psalm 115:4–7.

In our society the choice seems to be between accepting God or atheism, and the Old Testament denunciation of "false gods" sounds scarcely relevant. Yet in fact every human being has a god, though he or she may not dignify it with that name. My god is that for which I live, to which I consider it worth dedicating my whole self and my energy, in which I place all my trust. Modern idolatry does not identify itself as readily as did that of pagan times, but it is none the less real. Other gods still complete for our allegiance with the one God. To recognize Yahweh as God is not so easy or self-evident as might at first sight seem. The challenge addressed in some of the psalms (e.g. Ps. 42:3), "Where is your God?" is still worth responding to.

The one historical event recalled in Psalm 95 is the hardness of heart the people showed in the desert (vss. 8–11). This is not cited as a revelation of the nature of God so much as the nature of sin, the consequences of not heeding God. The psalm ends on this ominous note, recalling the rejection of the sinful generation in the desert. The ending, in fact, seems rather abrupt, but it is a well-chosen moment to leave the rest to silence. We are left with the echo of the frightening extent of human responsibility: we cannot but live with the consequences of our actions.

Personal experience of God's goodness

The patterns manifested in God's action on behalf of his chosen people appear also in the individual's experience of God. There are a number of psalms that sound like personal testimony to what God has been in the lives of individuals, either as he is manifested in a consistent pattern of action, or in some particular event. Sometimes in the Bible (and in psalms such as Pss. 9–10 and Ps. 102) prayers or expressions that sound very individual are ascribed to the nation as a whole, praying or speaking as a single voice. A striking example is Exodus 17:3, where the people, faced with death by thirst in the desert, complain to Moses: "Why did you bring *us* out of Egypt. . . Was it so that *I* could die of thirst, *my* children too, and *my* cattle?" This makes it difficult ever to describe any psalm with full confidence as an "individual" prayer. However, I shall be content to treat any psalm at its face value in this respect, and if it sounds individual, to treat it as the prayer of an individual.

The 23rd is one of the best known and most loved of all the psalms. Its popularity is partly due to its sentiments of peaceful trust and joy, and partly to its appealing pastoral imagery:

> In meadows of green grass he lets me lie,
> to the waters of rest he leads me,
> there he refreshes my throat (*nephesh*). (vs. 2)

In ancient Near Eastern texts it is not unusual for the king to be described as shepherd of his people, and ultimately Yahweh is the only king his people can recognize unreservedly (cf. 1 Sam. 7:4–9; Ps. 80:1). The title is also applied to the Messiah, the anointed king who shepherds Israel as Yahweh's vice-regent (cf. Jer. 23:1–6).

Psalm 23 is not completely unaware of the shadow side of life, but faces it with serene confidence with a sense of Yahweh as shepherd:

> Though I pass through the valley of death,
> I fear no harm.
> You are there with your crook and your staff,
> to give me comfort. (vs. 4)

Verses 5–6 abandon the shepherd image:

> You prepare a table for me
> in the sight of my foes.
> You anoint my head with oil
> my cup brims over. . . .

Oil for the ancients was the base for scents, and appreciation of the perfume enabled them to overlook the inconveniences of being anointed with oil that spring so readily to our tidy minds.

In praying Psalm 23 we should not expect that its sentiments, admirable and beautiful as they are, will always resonate with the movements of our own hearts, where the most evident sentiments may, at any given moment, be much less consoling. To feel obliged to pray Psalm 23 with enthusiasm simply because it is always recognized as beautiful leads us into the trap of formalized and unreal prayer.

Psalm 34 is an alphabetical psalm of joy in the discovery that Yahweh is on the side of the poor, the humble, the downtrodden (vs. 6); those whose spirit is crushed (vs. 18). The psalmist's proclamation will bring joy to the "humble" (vs. 2). He invites anyone who wishes to "taste and see how good the Lord is" (vs. 8). His confidence in Yahweh's protection is not unrealistic. The virtuous man will know hardship (vs. 19), but will not be overwhelmed by it.

Psalm 91 also proclaims Yahweh's protection of the man who trusts in him in a series of telling images: the man who trusts will be freed from snares (vs. 3), protected by Yahweh's outstretched wings (vs. 4), spared the fate of thousands falling all round him (vs. 7), immune from plague (vs. 10), spared hurt by the care of angels (vss. 11–12), and able to brave savage beasts and poisonous snakes (vs. 13). Such images make the psalm more memorable than Psalm 34, yet they lack some of the more sobering realism of that psalm.

Psalm 92 rejoices in God's achievements and the "depth" of his thoughts, which will not be evident to the wicked. (vs. 5–6). One is reminded of the transports of Romans 11:33–36, where Paul rejoices even at the very inscrutability of God's ways:

> How rich are the depths of God, how deep his wisdom and knowledge, how impossible to penetrate his motives, or understand his ways! Who could ever know the mind of the Lord, who could ever be his counselor? Who could ever give him anything or lend him anything? All that exists comes from him; all is by him and for him. To him be glory for ever! Amen.

One does not, of course, always feel this kind of delight in the darkness of God's inscrutability, but it does express a high state of delight in God. The psalmist in Psalm 92 is filled, moreover, with a great confidence in his ultimate triumph over the wicked; his is a state of high exultation.

Psalm 52, perhaps a little more soberly, expresses this same sense of security in God and ultimate triumph over the wicked, whose fate is assured:

> I for my part, like an olive tree
> growing in the house of God
> put my trust in God's love
> for ever and ever. (vs. 8)

Psalm 121 is also a personal testimony that "help comes to me from Yahweh, who made heaven and earth" (vs. 2).

The experience of God, which is hymned in Psalm 103, is especially the experience of forgiveness, closely linked with physical healing:

> Bless Yahweh, my throat (*nephesh*)
> and remember all his kindnesses:
> in forgiving all your offenses,
> in curing all your diseases,
> in redeeming your life from the Pit,
> in crowning you with love and tenderness,
> in filling your years with prosperity,
> in renewing your youth like an eagle's. (vss. 2–5)

The connection between physical and spiritual well-being is natural to Hebrew thought, where man is seen as such an integrated being; we shall consider it later in more detail.

God's punishment of sin is accepted, but pales into insignificance beside his tenderness:

> Yahweh is tender and compassionate,
> slow to anger, most loving.
> His indignation does not last forever,
> his resentment exists a short time only;
> he never treats us, never punishes us,
> as our guilt and our sins deserve. (vss. 8–10)

Once again Yahweh's concern for the downtrodden is praised as a manifestation of his justice:

> Yahweh works justice and judgment
>   for the oppressed. (vs. 6)

Ps. 116 thanks God for sparing the psalmist's life:

> Death's cords were tightening around me,
>   the nooses of Sheol,
> distress and anguish gripped me,
>   I invoked the name of Yahweh. (vss. 3–4)
> He has rescued me from death, my eyes from tears
>   and my feet from stumbling. (vs. 8)

This experience gives the psalmist hope even when he is aware of the deceitfulness of man (vss. 10–11). He intends to proclaim God's saving deed by sacrifice (vss. 13, 17–19).

Psalm 138 also thanks God for a particular instance of his saving help (vs. 3), which manifests his concern for the humble (vs. 6). The psalmist can live under threatening circumstances with the confidence that his experience has given him (vs. 7).

Welcoming God's judgment

Psalm 96 repeats many of the themes of Psalm 95. God's deeds are recalled, but not in specific detail (vs. 3). The contrast is drawn again between Yahweh and other gods (vss. 4–5); his kingship is demonstrated in his act of creation (vs. 10). Verses 11–13 call upon all creation to greet God's coming as judge with joy.

This may ring a little hollow in the ears of modern Christians, who are inclined to feel threatened by the prospect of being subjected to the judgment of God. Scripture certainly describes God as decreeing severe sentences on evildoers; we have been confronted with this in Psalm 95:10–11 and it will appear again in Psalm 59. Yet the underlying conviction is that God's intervention in the world is for good. Amos 4:6–12 describes God afflicting his people with quite terrible punishments, yet their purpose is evidently to bring them back to him; only repeated and stubborn refusal to respond to these initiatives will force God to bring down extreme punishment. Amos 7:1–9 shows God easily dissuaded from punishment. In Psalm 96 even inanimate creation is described as exultant that the will of God is to be put into effect, recalling Romans 8:18–25, where Paul envisages all of subhuman creation longing for deliverance from the frustration and futility to which human sinfulness condemns it.

Some of our modern unease with the idea of God's judgment can stem from a healthy realization of our own sinfulness as expressed in Psalm 130:

> If you never overlooked our sins, Yahweh,
> Lord, could anyone survive?
> But you do forgive us,
> and for that we revere you. (vss. 3–4)

But we also have a deep-seated fear that God has plans that bode ill for us, and for this there is no scriptural basis whatever. God's punishments are either a stratagem to bring about the repentance of the sinner, as in the texts referred to in Amos, or the consequences of a self-destructive course chosen by the sinner and obstinately pursued, as in Psalm 95:10–11. John's comment on the purpose and consequences of God's sending his Son into the world is true of every one of God's interventions in the world:

> God sent his son into the world,
> not to condemn the world,
> but so that through him the world might be saved.
> No one who believes in him will be condemned,
> but whoever refuses to believe is condemned already. . . .
> (Jn. 3:17–18).

Verse 13 in Psalm 96 claims that God will judge with "justice and truth"; this probably does little to calm our fears. In the Western world an ideal of justice, drawn from Roman law and mythology, is symbolized by a blindfolded female figure holding a drawn sword in one hand and a finely poised balance in the other. The impression is of impersonal equity and evenhandedness. God's justice as conceived by the Hebrew mind is rather different. God is "just" by being "true to himself"—hence "justice" is paired with "truth." This means that God will be faithful to his promises, and that he will, in accordance with his nature, be totally on the side of the underprivileged and the downtrodden (cf. Ps. 103:6). He judges in their favor (Ps. 10:18) the father of the orphan and the widow (Ps. 68:5). In Psalm 72 the king who shares in the justice of God himself will "uprightly defend the poorest, he will save the children of those in need, and crush their oppressors" (vs. 4). This is not an impersonal and impartial justice, but a quality of passionate concern for the downtrodden. Submitting oneself to this kind of justice has a quite different nature from submitting oneself to the frightening processes of impersonal justice.

We may still not immediately be able to share in the joyous anticipation that the author of Psalm 96 thinks is the natural reaction to the prospect of God's coming to judge us. Our fears can reveal to us something of our image of God, which may well be that of an ogre we have constructed in our own image and likeness.

Psalm 97 repeats the basic theme of joy at God's coming to judge. His coming is manifested in the thunderstorm, with some of the characteristics of a volcanic eruption (vs. 5). He shows his lordship over other gods (vss. 7, 9).

Psalm 99 expresses the tension that exists between belief in Yahweh as a loving and beneficent God and acknowledgment of his implacable opposition to sin. Yahweh is envisaged "enthroned above the cherubs"—that is, above the ark of the covenant in the temple (cf. vss. 1, 5, 9). He is the God who punishes and forgives (vs. 8). Even the classical statement of God's forgiving nature (Ex. 34:6–7) cannot ignore the paradox:

> Yahweh, a God of tenderness and compassion,
> slow to anger, rich in kindness and faithfulness.
> For thousands he maintains his kindness,
> forgives faults, transgression, sin;
> yet he lets nothing go unchecked,
> punishing the father's fault in the sons
>   and in the grandsons
> to the third and fourth generation. (Ex. 34:6–7)

Faced with this paradox, the psalmist takes courage from the memory of three great intercessors: Moses (e.g. Ex. 33:12–17); Aaron (Num. 17:6–15) and Samuel (1 Sam. 12:24). God's readiness to be moved by intercession shows his compassion triumphing over his anger. In Exodus 32:10 it is as though Yahweh realizes that he will never be able to resist Moses' intercession and begs to be left alone to give full reign to his anger:

> And now leave me alone, so that my anger may blaze out against
> them and devour them.

Moses nonetheless intervenes, and God's anger is turned aside, leading to the proclamation of Yahweh's forgiving nature in Exodus 34:6–7.

Fear of the Lord

Psalm 111, like Psalm 145, is an alphabetical psalm—each line beginning with the succeeding letter of the Hebrew alphabet. The psalm juxtaposes God's mercy (vs. 4), his faithfulness (vs. 5), and his inexorable power, which inspires the special fear that is the height (rather than "the beginning") of wisdom (vs. 10). This "fear of Yahweh" is not abject terror before a God who is malevolent, capricious, or unpredictable. It is a deep respect for and acknowledgment of his lordship. It can be compared with the way in which we recognize and have a healthy respect for the law of gravity. To the person who lives with an awareness and recognition of the force of gravity this poses no threat, but to attempt to ignore it breeds disaster. God is ready to forgive (cf. vs. 4) and so need not be feared as a vindictive force; yet to choose to go against him is as destructive as ignoring the law of gravity. God's absolute and total lordship is part of the way things are. We sometimes rebel against the way things are, but this is an ill-fated rebellion that does not change the way things are, and ultimately harms us.

Psalm 75 rejoices in God and expresses satisfaction with the way things are—in particular, confidence that there is a discernible justice at work in reality: the rebellion of the wicked is doomed to failure:

> For not from the east nor from the west,
> and not from the desert comes triumph,
> but it is God who executes judgment,
> putting down one and lifting up another . . .
> I will rejoice forever,
> I will sing the praises of the God of Jacob,
> all the horns of the wicked he will cut off,
> but the horns of the righteous shall be lifted up.
> (vss. 6–7, 9–10)

We do not always see the order and justice in things so clearly, or feel so enthusiastic about the way things are, and some psalms express confusion or dissatisfaction with the order of things. Psalm 73 relates the experience of a person for whom the question provoked a crisis of faith, and we shall later consider a number of psalms that reflect the difficulty we sometimes find in accepting the way things are. So, although the experience of Psalm 75, with its serene conviction that "God's in his heaven and all's right with the world" sounds very desirable, the opposite experience can also be assimilated into a real and living relationship with God.

Psalm 127 is in the form of a reflection rather than a prayer addressed directly to God. The psalmist reflects on the ultimate futility of human "busyness." Without God's favor human effort is fruitless, while he provides for his favored ones while they sleep (vss. 1–2).

Extreme effort may or may not be successful; success may or may not be enduring. Monuments to human achievement and genius, which have in fact survived for millennia, could have been wiped out by accidents of circumstance.

This psalm does not suggest conclusions, but is content to confront us with the facts as a basic law of reality. We may be inclined to rail against them for "unfairness," though one gets the impression that the psalmist finds them cause for satisfaction. We could conclude "What's the use," though the psalm does not. The psalm does not even deny that effort and personal investment of energy can produce great results; it simply warns us that it does not necessarily work out that way. Being brought up against this stubborn and sometimes galling law of reality can deepen our sense of what "fear of the Lord" means: recognition and, to the best of our ability, acceptance of the underlying law of reality—God's lordship.

Verses 3–5 reflect an agricultural society in a world much simpler than ours, where numerous offspring could be regarded as an unmixed blessing—a way of assuring individuals of unquestioning supporters, of standing in their community, of support in their old age, and of a sense that they will leave something tangible of themselves behind. These provide the best answer the psalmist knows to the sense of fleetingness expressed in verses 1–2. Even in our complicated urban society and overcrowded world we can find within ourselves remnants of the deeply human longing to leave descendants behind. Thus Psalm 127 can be the occasion that brings some of these sentiments—perhaps usually ignored or suppressed—to light. We can benefit from consciously incorporating them into our lives. This may mean nothing more than a heightened awareness of a little-explored corner of our hearts. We may become aware of previously unacknowledged opportunities in our lives to satisfy our human longing to nurture life.

Ritual exultation

There are a number of psalms that seem to have been written for some public ritual expressing joy and exultation in Yahweh.

Psalm 66 celebrates some particular experience of God's blessing, putting the particular instance into the context of all God's benefits on behalf of his people. Thus verses 1–12 call on creation to praise God for his care of his people, especially in saving them from the Egyptians.

> Come and see what God has done,
> he is terrible in his deeds among men.
> He turned the sea into dry land;
> men passed through the river on foot...
> (vss. 5–6)

Later, attention is focused less clearly on the one event of Exodus, and the thanksgiving comes to be expressed in terms that could apply to any one of Israel's experiences of being saved from the hands of enemies:

> You tested us, God,
> you refined us like silver,
> you let us fall into the net,
> you laid a heavy burden on us,
> you let men ride over our heads,
> we went through fire and through water,
> but now you have brought us forth into abundance.
> (vss. 10–12)

The psalmist now announces his intention of offering thanksgiving sacrifices, as he had vowed in time of distress (vss. 13–15), and although it would be possible to suppose that this is a continuation of thanksgiving for Exodus or God's other saving interventions in history, verses 16–19 make more sense if they are understood as proclamation of a personal favor received from God. Thanksgiving, as is usual, involves a brief reliving of the experience for which the psalmist is giving thanks.

Verse 18 says, literally, "If I had *seen* (or "looked at") guilt in my heart, Yahweh would not have listened." Does the psalmist think that the fact that Yahweh rescued him proves that he was innocent and blameless all along? The psalms usually admit that God will rescue the sinner from the consequences of his guilt. Psalm 103 was just such a confession that God had rescued the psalmist from the sickness that was the manifestation of his guilt. Yet there is a shift of attitude required of the sinner before this healing can take place. Psalm 32 suggests that what is required is an acknowledgment of sin for what it is; as long as the psalmist kept silence he suffered; admitting his guilt opened the way for the Lord to forgive (vss. 3–5). Psalm 18:24–27 also suggests that the dishonest man cannot experience God's justice; he will discover only his own dishonesty reflected back on himself:

> Faithful you are with the faithful,
> blameless with the blameless,
> pure with one who is pure,
> but crafty with the devious. (vss. 25–26)

If the poet of Psalm 66 is in line with this tradition, Verse 18 must mean something like: "If I looked with complacency on sin in my heart, the Lord would not have listened," or, as the Revised Standard Version translates: "If I had cherished sin in my heart, the Lord would not have listened." The psalmist is filled with gratitude that God heard his prayer, and does not take it for granted as a right:

> Blessed be God,
> who did not ignore my prayer,
> nor withhold his love from me (vs. 20)

Psalm 24 seems to have been composed for use in a procession. Verses 7–10 are in a dialogue form, seemingly between a group outside the city or temple demanding entrance (vss. 7, 9): the latter demanding the credentials of whoever seeks to enter (vss. 8, 10), to be answered by the former group with a proclamation of Yahweh who seeks to enter: "the strong, the valiant, the valiant in battle, the king of glory" (vss. 8, 10).

We can reconstruct the scene from our knowledge of customs connected with the ark of the covenant, that portable, boxlike structure with the statues of cherubs on top described in Exodus 25:10–22. The empty space above the cherubs was regarded as the place of God's special presence (Ex. 25:22). During the time of wandering in the desert this portable shrine of God's presence led the wandering people (Ex. 40:36–38; Num. 10:35–36), and at a later period the ark accompanied the army into battle, a tangible sign and pledge of the presence of God among them (cf. 1 Sam. 4:1–11). Psalm 24 would be a fitting accompaniment for the triumphant return of the ark from battle, or the ritual reenactment of such occasions by a ceremonial procession of the ark.

God's mighty power is manifested not only in his victory over the enemies of his people, but also in his constant victory over the destructive waters of chaos:

> To Yahweh belong earth and all it holds,
> the world and all who live in it;
> he himself founded it on the ocean,
> based it firmly on the nether sea. (vss. 1–2)

The psalm also includes a reflection on what is required of one who wishes to be admitted into the presence of God: he must be "clean of hands and pure of heart" (vss. 3–4). This suggests that he must be quit of obligations arising from past actions ("clean of hands") and interiorly transformed in the way that is the only guarantee of effective conversion ("pure of heart"). He does not "lift his throat to what is worthless," or, in other words, look for fulfillment to false gods, nor "swear to a lie." These verses recall Psalm 15, which we shall consider later on.

Psalm 118 has some similarities with Psalm 24, being a song of triumph of a victorious warrior returning to Jerusalem, with occasional responses from the welcoming party:

> vss. 1–3: the warrior calls on the crowds to join in celebration.
> vss. 4–14: reliving of the battle.
> vs. 19: the victor addresses the welcoming party and
>   demands entry.
> vss. 20: response of the welcoming party.
> vss. 21–22: triumphant city of the warrior.
> vss. 23–27: response of welcoming party.
> vss. 28–29: triumphant cry of warrior.

The exact division between the parts belonging to the two "choirs" is not always quite certain, but the general nature of the psalm is clear.

In Christian thought the ultimate triumph of God is Christ's victory over death at his resurrection and glorification. Both Psalms 24 and 18 can easily be used as a vividly imagined picture of the triumphant Christ claiming entry into heavenly glory.

Beyond words
The psalms we have been considering in this chapter so far have expressed joy in God either because of his deeds, recalled more or less explicitly, or because of his attributes, which summarize certain constant patterns of his activity. Words, however, always fall short, and there are some psalms that simply express joy in God, without any

attempt to explain just why their authors feel this joy; they tell us what it is like, but do not attempt to explain why they feel it.

Psalm 131 expresses a contentment in God that goes beyond thought and understanding, a wordless enjoyment of security in him. It rejoices in the respite—perhaps shortlived—from seeking answers, explanations, systems:

> Yahweh, my heart has no lofty ambitions
> my eyes do not look too high.
> I am not concerned with great affairs,
> nor marvels beyond my scope.
> Enough for me to keep my soul tranquil and quiet
> like a child in its mother's arms,
> as content as a child that has been weaned. (vss. 1–2)

This is the state of Job when, after long, anguished, and embittered searching and casting about for answers, he suddenly discovers that he does not want to ask questions any more:

> I am the man who has been obscuring your designs
> with my empty-headed words . . .
> I knew you then only by hearsay, but now, having
> seen you with my own eyes,
> I retract all I have said, and in dust and ashes
> I repent. (Job 42:3.5–6)

We cannot renounce thought or the search for explanations and meaning. Yet ultimately none of our explanations, no matter how brilliant, is totally satisfying, and ultimate peace comes by going beyond questioning. For most of us, as for Job, there is no short cut to this state. We cannot attain it simply by choosing not to search or to question. It is only when the mind has reached the end of its competence and been reduced to silence that we can experience the peace that goes beyond words. At least for most people that wordless peace will not become a habitual state, though it is something we can train ourselves to become more adept at getting in touch with. Moreover, the experience of this peace, though not itself continuous, can overflow and affect other states of consciousness.

Psalm 16, despite the initial petition, "Look after me, God, I take refuge in you" (vs. 1), is a psalm of delight in God. It is not exactly wordless delight, but though the psalmist expresses it at some length, he is more concerned to tell us how he feels than to explain why he feels that way. Yahweh is his heritage, and he feels that it is a very satisfactory lot: the measuring lines used to apportion the land, which is the basis of wealth in an agricultural society, have been good to him, since his lot is Yahweh (vs. 5). This may mark the psalmist as a Levite, a member of the tribe which at an early date lost its claim to tribal territory and instead specialized in the service of the sanctuary, and whose inheritance was Yahweh, not land.

Those who serve other gods are laying up sorrow for themselves; the service of Yahweh is a joy, which, in keeping with the Hebrew approach to the human person, he experiences in a very bodily way:

> My heart exults, my liver rejoices,
> even my flesh will rest in safety,
> for you will not abandon my throat to Sheol. (vs. 9)

The exultant psalmist in Psalm 134 calls on the "night watch" of the temple to praise God, as though, impatient with the limitations of his own human capacity for praise, he wants to make others' praise his own. This can possibly degenerate into an almost superstitious shuffling of one's individual responsibility onto the shoulders of others, or an unrealistic expectation that others live up to ideals to which one pays only lip service oneself. But it can also express generous desires outstripping one's own capabilities, and awareness that each individual's living finds its place within a common human enterprise.

Delight in the will of God

A particular form of delight in God is delight in his will, and in the psalms this often takes the form of praise of his law. One can observe a law simply because it is imposed and transgression will bring punishment. There will be nothing very joyful or enlivening about this kind of observance; it is experienced as constraint, to which one reacts by resentment and deep-seated, even if repressed, rebellion. A written law can, however, reveal to a person a way of living that corresponds to his or her deepest longings; it can enable them to discover the law written in their hearts. In this case living by the law is joyful and enlivening.

It is obviously the latter kind of experience that is described in the psalms praising God's law. "The Law" to the psalmists meant, of course, the law of Moses contained in Exodus 20:1–23:19; Exodus 25 to the end of the book of Leviticus and Numbers 1:1–10:10, and the legal sections of the book of Deuteronomy (Deut. 4–26). Closer study of this complex mass of prescriptions reveals that we are dealing not with one single mass of laws, but with several different collections of law, drawn up in response to the needs of the people of Israel at different times. The earliest collection seems to be the so-called "book of the covenant" (Ex. 20:22–23:19). The book of Deuteronomy is based on this, reworking parts of it and making additions in the light of the needs of the late seventh century B.C. Still later, Leviticus 17–26 was drawn up, to codify and organize the sacrificial worship of Israel and the complicated system of taboos governing fitness to participate in it. Finally, during the Babylonian exile, therefore during the sixth century B.C. Leviticus 17–26 was taken over and completed by a mass of ritual laws known as the "priestly" law. The Ten Commandments (Ex. 20:1–17 and the slightly later edition of Deut. 5:6–22) is a separate compendium of simple rules of conduct, which in some form or other seems to have existed from earliest times. Some would even say that the book of the covenant and the book of Deuteronomy are very expanded elaborations of the Ten Commandments.

The Old Testament presents this complicated mass of laws as revealed directly by God to Moses. This is a vivid and dramatic way of conveying the authors' conviction that these laws do express God's will for his people, but it also gives the impression that what is prescribed or forbidden is eternally and irrevocably binding for no discernible reason other than an inscrutable and unexplained decision of God. The law is in danger of becoming something more than an attempt to express an understanding of what God was asking of his people and becomes as sacred and unquestionable as God himself. It is all too easy for the individual to abdicate the personal responsibility of truly listening to God who speaks in and through the movements of the human heart and simply to follow instructions.

Reflection on this hidden weakness of an idolatrous esteem for the law became critical when Christianity won numbers of gentile converts. Many prescriptions of the law appealed to nothing more than the Jewish sense of national identity, prescribing customs by which the

Jews delighted in demonstrating their difference from the gentiles. Jews could indeed measure pride in their Jewishness in zealous avoidance of pagan fashion by "not cutting the corners of their hair" (Lev. 19:27). The practice of circumcision gave the Jews a defiant sense of being "different," but to gentiles the practice seemed barbaric and disgusting. Paul insisted in the strongest terms that Christians were not bound by any written code, but followed the prompting of the Spirit poured out in their hearts. This in fact is in keeping with the truest Old Testament understanding of the law, as expressed, for example, in Jeremiah 31:31–34:

> See, the days are coming—it is Yahweh who speaks—when I will make a new covenant with the house of Israel and the house of Judah, but not a covenant like the one I made with their ancestors on the day I took them by the hand to lead them out of the land of Egypt . . . Deep within them I will plant my Law, writing it on their hearts. Then I will be their God and they shall be my people . . .

We all have somewhere within us a hope that one day someone will write a set of instructions for living that will be absolutely foolproof and that will relieve us of the frightening responsibility of our own lives. Looked at superficially, the psalms praising God's law may sometimes seem to express and approve this longing. But when experience has shown us how illusory this hope is, we can return to these psalms and pray them as an expression of longing for and delight in the only truly effective guide—the movement of God's breathing in our hearts. If we have some experience of what this means we can pray such psalms with real joy; if not, they are a pious sham.

Psalm 19 exults in the law of God as perfect, giving life, joy, and light—more attractive than finest gold and more delicious than honey (vss. 7–10). This praise of the law follows directly on the hymn of praise to God the creator, especially as his power is manifested in the sun, which we have already considered (vss. 1–6). The two themes may seem at first hardly related, but perhaps the psalmist feels that the harmony and beauty that is manifested in material creation is manifested likewise in human life when it is lived subject to that same creative wisdom and power that is so spectacularly manifested in the sun. Opening oneself to the will of God means opening oneself to that force whose power to create life and beauty is evident in the universe.

Even as he is joyfully aware of how good it is for him to be formed by the will of God, the psalmist is vaguely aware of resistances in himself to God's creative action. No amount of human effort or self-examination can purge this out of him; he prays to be cleansed of that sinfulness which lies deeper than any human self-examination or effort can reach:

> But who can detect his own failings?
> Wash out my hidden faults,
> and from pride restrain your servant,
> never let it dominate me.
> So shall I be above reproach,
> free from grave sin. (vss. 12–13)

The psalmist does not think that the good life consists simply in adjusting his conduct to meet the prescriptions of the law. He longs for a deeper healing than that. Moreover, for him God's action is not directed simply at controlling his life and preventing sin. His intuition of the exuberant power of God manifested in the universe lets him dare hope that, if he gives himself over to God, he will have something of the beauty and exultant might of the sun.

Psalm 1 is much less exuberant, a simple reflection on the consequences of living according to God's will. The man who so lives

> . . . is like a tree that is planted by water streams,
> yielding its fruit in season, its leaves never fading,
> success attends all he does. (vs. 3)

In contrast with the green, leafy, well-watered image of the friend of God, the fate of the wicked is described in terms of dessication:

> (The wicked) are like chaff blown away by the wind,
> the wicked shall not stand firm when judgment comes.
> (vss. 4–5)

A metaphorical description of the happiness of the good man and the fate of the wicked does not cause many problems; one interprets the metaphor as one sees fit.

Psalm 112, however, is more problematic. Like Psalm 1 it proclaims the joy of knowing and doing God's will:

> Happy the man who fears Yahweh,
> by joyfully keeping his commandments. (vs. 1)

However, the poet expects that this happiness will take well-defined and clearly discernible forms:

> Children of such a man will be powers on earth,
> descendants of the upright will always be blessed.
> There will be riches and wealth for his family,
> and his righteousness can never change. (vss. 2–3)

Psalm 128 has similar hopes for the good man:

> Happy are those who fear Yahweh
>   and follow in his paths.
> You will eat what your hands have worked for.
> Your wife: a fruitful vine within your house.
> Your sons: round your table like shoots
> round an olive tree. (vss. 1–4)

Our response to this may well be a rather bitter laugh: life is not like that. We may even feel that our cynicism expresses a higher kind of wisdom, a realism compared with the naive trust expressed in Psalms 112 and 128. We may even appeal to the example of Jesus to show that the just man cannot expect anything but suffering in the world as it is.

There is a great deal of satisfying self-righteousness and self-pity in telling ourselves and the world, "I've tried my hardest, spared no effort, left nothing undone—and it hasn't turned out right; my family life is a mess, my friends have abandoned me, and I'm still not happy." We are capable of programming ourselves to try hard and fail, and prove the world wrong by putting it in the wrong. That absolves us from any further effort, and gives us the right to retire to our armchair as disillusioned critics of anyone who wants to reform or transform the world. "It can't be done. I've tried everything and nothing works."

If the rather naive optimism of these two psalms exposes by contrast this kind of cynicism, it has opened up for us the way to healing. Our self-defeating cynicism becomes so ingrained and so colors our world view that very often we cannot see any way of changing. But, as some of the psalms prayed from a condition of sinfulness will show us, accepting responsibility for what is wrong with our lives is itself a healing of no small importance, and can open up a way to healing that we never thought existed.

The longest psalm of all—Psalm 119—is concerned with joy and delight in the law of the Lord, each verse in the successive sections beginning with the succeeding letter of the Hebrew alphabet. It is often hard to see any logical progression. A fairly limited number of sentiments are expressed over and over again, without much evidence of order—the poet's main concern was probably to find a sentence beginning with the right letter of the alphabet. Those who keep the law are happy (vss. 1–2). God's law is the governing force in the universe (vss. 89–91); it is right and reliable (vss. 137–138), and unchanging (vs. 152). More personally, the psalmist finds joy in the law:

> "In the way of your decrees lies my joy,
>   a joy beyond wealth" (vs. 14);
> "I find delight in your statues, I do not
>   forget your word" (vs. 16);
> "Your commandments fill me with delight,
>   I love them deeply" (vs. 47);
> "Your word is a lamp to my feet, a light
>   on my path" (vs. 105);
> "Your decrees are my eternal heritage,
>   they are the joy of my heart" (vs. 111);
> "I hate, I detest delusion. Your law is
>   what I love" (vs. 163).

He also knows what it is to cling to Yahweh's decrees in time of difficulty:

> "Though anguish and distress grip me,
>   your commandments are my delight" (vs. 143);
> "Though smoked dry as a wineskin,
>   I do not forget your statues" (vs. 83).

These prayers can sound smug and self-satisfied, almost self-congratulatory. But they are interspersed with other expressions of the difficulty of really knowing God's law, where the psalmist recognizes his own sinful lack of understanding of God's will and prays for enlightenment and inspiration. He has enough insight into and experience of doing the will of God to know the joy that it gives, and to long for fuller experience of this joy:

> "You yourself have made your precepts known,
>   to be faithfully kept.
> Oh, may my behavior be constant in keeping
>   your statutes" (vss. 4–5);
> "I have sought you with all my heart,
>   do not let me stray from your
>   commandments" (vs. 10).

To know God's will it is necessary to do more than simply read the law:

> "Open my eyes, I shall concentrate on the
>   marvels of your law.
> Exile though I am on earth,
>   do not hide your commandments from me" (vss. 18–19).
> Turn me from the path of delusion,
>   grant me the grace of your law" (vs. 29).

At times he admits former lawlessness:

> "Down in the dust I lie prostrate,
>   revive me as your word has guaranteed.
> I admitted my behavior, you answered me,
>   now teach me your statutes" (vss. 25–26).
> "In earlier days I had to suffer, I used to stray,
>   now I remember your promise" (vs. 67).
> "It was good for me to have to suffer,
>   the better to learn your statutes" (vs. 71).

Very frequently he prays for deliverance from enemies who could turn him away from devotion to God's will:

> "Endlessly the arrogant have jeered at me,
>   but I have not swerved from your law" (vs. 51).
> "Though the arrogant tell foul lies about me,
>   I wholeheartedly respect your precepts . . .
> "How much longer has your servant to live,
>   when will you condemn my persecutors?"
> "The arrogant have dug pitfalls for me in
>   defiance of your law . . ."
> "Though these wretches have almost done for me,

I have never abandoned your precepts."
"Lovingly intervene, give me life,
    and I will observe your decrees" (vss. 84–88).

Such prayer needs to be faced with particular honesty. It seems so "right" to rejoice in the law of God that we may not want to admit even to ourselves any discordant feelings. To rebel against the idea of "God's law" may not be a sign of our innate wickedness, but a sign of longing to advance beyond a religion of external controls and to hear the life-giving voice of God himself.

Psalm 101 expresses delight in the will of God, but in a different way. It does not praise the law, but eagerly expresses an intention of living in God's way henceforth. It is meant as a prayer for the king, and some of the resolutions make sense in the light of this: it is obviously particularly desirable that the king not give ear to slanderers (vs. 5), nor let hypocrites profit from their dishonesty by rising to high places in the court (vs. 7). Still, we can find some personal relevance: we are all inclined to let other people form our opinions for us, or to favor people who tell us what we want to hear. The resolution to banish the wicked (vs. 8) is hardly literally applicable.

There is a suspicion of self-righteousness and self-satisfaction about the psalm. Perhaps we are not meant to pray it without some qualms, and if we listen to the qualms we feel we could begin to get in touch with God's response to our prayer.

Psalm 133 also rejoices in the goodness of God's will, but in a simpler, less sanctimonious way. The author has simply experienced the solid goodness of brotherly love and voices his satisfaction in prayer:

How good and how pleasant it is,
brothers dwelling in unity (vs. 1).

7 ❖

Prayer in Desolation

Human life is many faceted. It contains darkness as well as light, pain as well as joy. We say "yes" to life and accept a package deal—or nothing at all. But we have all sorts of ways of attempting to narcotize ourselves against the painful in life, ranging from crass flights into pleasure or oblivion to the most subtle and devious ways to deny suffering. The religious person is no less subject to such temptation than anyone else. Stoicism keeps reappearing in religious guise, as though it were somehow more virtuous to pretend that suffering does not really trouble us. Puritanism is perhaps even more seductive—as though we could avoid suffering by never really enjoying anything.

Many of the psalms were born out of painful experience—not just of pain borne uncomplainingly for God's sake, but of pain keenly felt as an imposition, of moments when pain seemed to obliterate even one's relationship with God. It is obviously religiously "proper" to rejoice in the Lord, or even to present one's petitions to him with decent moderation; it is not so obviously right to "pour out one's heart to God" when it would be an outpouring of anger, bitterness, and rebellion. Yet this is what the psalms practice.

Throughout life the existence of pain in our lives is denied by others. We are told "It's all right!" In other words, our pain is an illusion. Or we are bullied into forgetting our pain by disapproval: "Don't wallow in it!" All this happens because, for most people, it is painful to see someone else in pain. Few of us are self-assured enough and sufficiently at peace with ourselves to share another person's suffering. We prefer to forget that people suffer, or harden ourselves to the sight of suffering, or pretend it is not there. Society conspires to deny suffering where possible.

The flight from what is painful—in our own or other people's lives—is a desperate and hopeless enterprise. Pain and suffering are part of human life, and we can begin to deal with them constructively only when we accept them. To try to deny our suffering adds another, this time self-inflicted, injury to the original cause of suffering. Deep down we are aware of this. We cannot really deceive ourselves. Somewhere we keep score, and a reservoir of unhealed pain and anger simmers away, influencing our outlook and our attitudes, and occasionally building up to an explosion of violence and bitterness that surprises even ourselves by its vehemence, and bears little relationship to whatever occasioned it.

There is no need for us to deny or dissemble our pain before God. He is big enough to cope with our experience of suffering and its expression, no matter how explosive it may be. Prayer is one of the few safe spaces where we can admit our suffering to ourselves and to another. This need not be just a nod to acknowledge the fact that we suffer; it can fruitfully involve being in suffering in the presence of God.

Lamentation is part of the Hebrew repertoire of prayer—expression of raw emotion almost unprocessed by the controlling and censoring forces of intellect and "conscience." This is not to say that the Hebrews were altogether immune from the temptation to cope by denial. We shall see, presently, examples of prayer where some such mechanism comes into play, but this is the exception rather than the rule.

Lamentations 3 is a particularly vivid example of this prayerful entering into the depths of bitter experience. Although the book of Lamentations is set against the time of the exile, when the chosen race had lost much of what they considered were pledges of God's love for them, Lamentations 3 is a very personal expression of anguish:

> I am the man familiar with misery under the rod of God's anger.
> I am the one he has driven and forced to walk
>   in darkness and without any light.
> Against me alone he turns his hand again and again,
>   all day long. (vss. 1–2)

This is a vivid expression of the feeling that one has been singled out for special suffering. Carried to extremes, this amounts to paranoia and, rationally, we can perhaps see that our suffering is never unique; we can even see that others suffer more than we. But the poet feels his situation as an utterly unparalleled disaster, and therefore express-es it as such.

The poet moves on from paranoid feelings to feelings of resentment against God, whose favor seems to have changed to indifference or even to enmity:

> He has walled me in; I cannot escape;
>> He has made my chains heavy,
>> and when I call and shout, he shuts out my prayer.
> He has blocked my ways with cut stones,
>> he has obstructed my paths,
> For me he has been a lurking bear, a lion on the watch . . .
> and I now say, "My strength is gone, the hope which came
>> from Yahweh." (vss. 7–10)

Willing though he is to listen to and express his emotions, rational or not as they may be, the poet does not renounce the human need to come to terms rationally with what has happened to him. He knows and expresses that state where the mind stubbornly turns an experi-ence over and over and seeks ineffectually but persistently to solve it by providing an answer:

> Brooding on my anguish and affliction is gall and wormwood.
> My spirit ponders it continually and sinks within me.
> This is what I shall tell my heart, and so recover hope:
>> "The favors of the Lord are not all past,
>> his kindnesses not exhausted. . . .
>> great is his faithfulness. (vss 19–23)

At this point the poet begins to feel that the answer may lie in stoic acceptance:

> It is good to wait in silence for Yahweh to save.
> It is good for a person to bear the yoke
> from youth upward,
>>> to sit in solitude and silence
>>> when the Lord fastens it on him,
>>> to put his lips to the dust—
>>> perhaps there is still hope—
>>> to offer his cheek to the smiter,

> to be overwhelmed by insults.
> For the Lord does not reject mankind forever and ever . . .
> he takes no pleasure in abasing and afflicting
>   the human race (vss. 26–33).

This may not be an attempt to deny suffering. Perhaps, having vented his emotions in verses 1–18, and sought some explanation of things for himself in verses 19–24, his emotions shade over into resignation in verses 25–29, and to real confidence in God in verses 30–39, leading him to awareness of sin in verses 40–41:

> Let us stretch out our hearts and hands to God
>   in heaven,
> We are the ones who have sinned,
>   who have rebelled,
> and you have not forgiven.

This leads him back to an awareness of suffering (vss. 43–54). This time round, the tone is less strident and the experience seemingly rather less keen than before.

Verses 55–66 mingle thanksgiving with petition for deliverance in a way that is at first rather confusing:

> Yahweh, I have called on your name from the deep pit,
> You heard me crying,
> Do not close your ear to my prayer.
> You came near the day I called to you,
> you said, "Do not be afraid,"
> You have defended the cause of my soul,
> you have redeemed my life,
> Yahweh, you have seen the wrong done to me;
> grant me redress.

The poet could be speaking of previous occasions when his prayers had been heard, which would give him hope that his present need was also known to God. But it is not unusual in prayers of desolation for the prayer to move from seemingly inconsolable grief to serene confidence, and even to thanksgiving (cf. Pss. 28; 31; 55; 57; 109). The sudden shift may seem unmotivated, and there have been various attempts to explain such a sudden change in mood within a single composition. Some have speculated that between the lamentation part of the prayer and the expression of confidence and thanksgiving, a priest or some other cult official assured the petitioner that his or her prayer had been heard. None of the psalms mentioned give any inkling of such a process, and I would rather see these psalms as reflections of a real movement of the human heart in prayer. If one is willing to enter completely into desolation in prayer, it is not unusual for the sense of desolation suddenly to yield to peace and assurance. It is as though one can reach calm only by setting course into the heart of the storm, or, to use another image, as if one can reach the calm, untroubled water in the depths of a well only by being willing to go through the disturbances in the upper levels. Having entered fully into his sense of desolation (vss. 1–18) and tried to explain it to himself (vss. 19–39) he is driven back first to a renewed awareness of his present predicament (vss. 40–54) and then into a sudden sense of peace (vss. 55–63).

Enemies and vindictive prayer in the psalms

Already Lamentations 3:64–66 raises an issue that often comes up in psalms of desolation by cursing the enemies who have brought disaster on Jerusalem:

> Yahweh, repay them as their deeds deserve.
> Give them hardness of heart,
> Your curse be on them.
> Pursue them in fury, root them out
> from underneath your heavens.

Enemies are frequently featured among causes of suffering in the psalms. Perhaps part of the reason for this is the Old Testament tendency to see suffering as a divinely ordained punishment for sin. Any person who suffers misfortune is judged to be suffering God's punishment, and so is revealed to all the word as a sinner. Hence friends become cool and enemies see themselves vindicated. Enemies may even seize upon the occasion to attack with new confidence, now that God is on their side.

Thus in Psalm 38 the basic cause of the psalmist's distress is sickness, described in verses 3–8. The consequence of his sickness is that he is abandoned by friends and attacked by his enemies (vss. 11–12). Psalm 69:7 describes how even his closest relatives become alienated when misfortune strikes. In Psalm 31, too, the basic trouble seems to be sickness (vs. 10), with subsequent gloating of enemies (vss. 11–13). In this kind of circumstance, one will be rescued from one's enemies only when the occasion of their attacks is removed. At other times, however, there is no theological pretext for the attacks of enemies, which are motivated only by ordinary human malice. In Psalm 35 enemies for no reason (vs. 7) lay snares and make false accusations about the psalmist (vs. 11), despite the fact that he has shown nothing but concern for them in their time of trouble (vss. 13–14). He prays that they may not be encouraged in their wickedness by being allowed to triumph (vss. 25–26). In Psalm 54:3 the attacks are manifestations of arrogance on the part of the psalmist's enemies; in Psalm 55:12–13 the psalmist has been betrayed by a friend and colleague; in Psalm 56:5–6 it is a malicious conspiracy to trap the psalmist in his speech. In Psalm 57:4–6 the psalmist's enemies lurk and plot to bring about his downfall, as is also the case in Psalm 59:3–4. No special motivation is suggested; the psalmist's enemies are acting out of their perverse nature.

In most of the psalms mentioned, the psalmist is content to ask to be delivered, or at most vindicated, in the eyes of his enemies. But there are times where the psalmist goes further. Psalm 109, for example, is almost totally concerned with elaborating in detail disasters that the psalmist wishes on his enemies (vss. 6–20). Certainly his enemies are in the wrong, at least as the psalmist sees it (vs 5), but their malevolence is returned with interest. Psalm 129 is less offensive, since it speaks in more metaphorical terms, but it still hopes that the psalmist's enemies will be like grass that grows on the roof and is doomed to wither quickly because of a lack of deep soil. Psalm 140 devotes most of its attention to begging for deliverance, but in verses 9–10 the psalmist turns on his persecutors and curses them. To further offend our sensibilities, in verses 12–13 he claims to feel confident that Yahweh will in fact wreak vengeance:

> I know that Yahweh will avenge the wretched
> and see justice done for the poor.
> The virtuous shall have good cause to thank your name,
> and the upright find a home in you.

We may be able to cope with the idea that God is on the side of the downtrodden, but we should prefer to see the downtrodden remain suitably humble, or at least patient, in their sufferings.

Perhaps the simplest way of dealing with this kind of prayer is to tell ourselves that it is an aspect of Old Testament spirituality that has been superseded by Christ, and then to ignore passages such as the above. However, the passages deserve more attention than this.

Christians are not exempt from anger, even if we imagine we should be. Even if we recognize that our anger is unjustified or unreasonable, it seldom suffices to defuse it, though it may well lead us to suppress it or to avoid acting on it. Experience shows, however, that even anger that has been banished and supposedly suppressed in the name of sweet reason, continues to smolder, and sometimes breaks out with all the more ferocity, and less appropriateness, when we have attempted to kill it. We imagine we have behaved in a Christian and rational way when provoked, only to find that stored-up anger eats us up. We explode with frightening ferocity at some tiny provocation. Or our anger turns inward and we are stricken with black depression. Even persons who have, at great cost to themselves, lived externally blameless lives, can find themselves eaten up, their vitality sapped and their joy lost, through this kind of displaced hostility. Do we have to accept this as a mysterious trial sent by God, to be endured with as much grace as possible?

This is a last resort. There are usually more ways of expressing anger when it comes up than we are aware of—rather than storing it up until it reaches explosive proportions. Just how this can be done is not my concern here, though it is everyone's concern in life. But there will still be occasions where there is no way of expressing anger, either because circumstances do not permit, or because others with whom we are dealing are not in a position to cope with it. I suggest that the vindictive passages in the psalms are examples of another constructive way to cope with our anger—express it to God. Some human beings are not always big enough to cope with even mild and reasonable expressions of anger, but God is big enough to absorb our small human hostilities. Certainly he will not be pressured into giving effect to our vindictive little wishes, no matter how urgently they may be expressed.

This may sound like a clever sleight of hand, saving the psalms from being convicted, but leaving some very real questions. Can one really claim that it is healthy to give rein to our vindictiveness, even in prayer? Would it not be better to acknowledge that we all have this side to our nature, without reinforcing it and seeming to give it legitimacy by expressing it in such loving detail? Has anyone who has ever prayed those vindictive passages in the psalms found himself or herself transformed by a sort of catharsis into a more peaceful person? Do the passages not open the way to the nastiest sort of vindictiveness—a vindictiveness that is religiously sanctioned, and where God is supposed to share in the dispositions of hatred felt by religious fanatics?

All this is a real danger. It is good to express our anger and vindictiveness to God provided this is a really prayerful experience—turning it over completely to him, and not just rehearsing it to ourselves. This implies a willingness to let go of our feelings, once they are expressed, and leave God to deal with the petitions prompted by vindictive emotion. Psalm 64 is a psalm against enemies, but it does not arouse the same sense of discomfort in us as, say, Psalm 109, because the psalmist very explicitly looks to God alone to deal with his enemies:

> God will shoot them with his own arrow,
> wound them without warning.
> He will destroy them for that tongue of theirs
> and all who see their fall will shake their heads.
> (vss. 7–8)

Or, as Psalm 62 attests:

> God has spoken once,
> twice have I heard this:
> it is for God to be strong,
> for you, Lord, to be loving,
> and you yourself repay
> a person as his works deserve. (vss. 11–12)

If we assume that it is legitimate to express our anger in prayer to God and dare to pray this type of psalm accordingly, then these psalms can serve as a startling revelation of the hostilities we harbor within, carefully suppressed and hidden even from ourselves. This can be a healing revelation. So long as we ourselves are deceived by the meek and mild image we present to the world our suppressed anger works in hidden ways. Our very meekness can be a subtle way of getting even with others. There is a very real satisfaction to be derived from dealing with others submissively, confirming us in a feeling of moral superiority and being a victim in life. It can even be a subtle way of twisting others to do our will. If we dare to pray the "violent" prayers of the psalms we may be dismayed to discover whom our imagination casts in the role of the enemy, and the depth and extent of our suppressed anger.

Finally, the psalms express only one side of a dialogue with God. As well as relinquishing our violent emotions to him, we must leave our hearts open to hear God's response. We should not too easily identify our shocked and conventionally pious reaction to the discovery of our anger with the voice of God. That is very likely to be no more than an echo of parents and mentors down through our lives who, as much for their own peace of mind as for any other reason, warned us that it was not "nice" to be angry, and pressed upon us the need to accept meekly their power over us. God's response to our anger will be healing, and will transform a destructive and self-defeating emotion into a positive power and driving force in our lives.

The punch line of the book of Jonah is a fragment of dialogue between an angry man and God. Having prophesied disaster for Nineveh, Jonah is described settling down to watch the outcome in comfort. He is distressed that the Ninevites seem to have responded well to his preaching and complains to God:

> "Ah, Yahweh! Is not this just as I said would happen when I was still at home? That is why I went and fled to Tarshish: I knew that you were a God of tenderness and compassion, slow to anger and rich in graciousness, relenting from evil. So now, Yahweh, please take away my life, for I might as well be dead as go on living." And Yahweh replied, "Are you right to be angry?"
>
> (vss. 2–3)

Later Jonah is distressed at the death of a castor oil plant that was providing him with shelter:

> Jonah was overcome and begged for death, saying, "I might as well be dead as go on living." God said to Jonah, "Are you right to be angry about the castor oil plant?" He replied, "I have every right to be angry, to the point of death." Yahweh replied "You

> are only upset about a castor oil plant which cost you no labor,
> which you did not make grow, which sprouted in a night and has
> perished in a night. And am I not to feel sorry for Nineveh, the
> great city, in which there are more than a hundred and twenty
> thousand people who cannot tell their right hand from their left,
> to say nothing of all the animals?" (vss. 8–11)

Jonah is, of course, something of a comic-book character, and his
childishness is immediately evident to us. But if the vindictive psalms
can flush our own childish indignation into the open and provoke such
dialogue in our lives, they will have served a noble purpose.

Prayer in national need

A first group of psalms in desolation is born out of national danger or
disaster. Sometimes the painful circumstances are more or less taken
for granted as a fairly normal fluctuation in the course of events, as
in Psalms 60, 80, or 108. There is still, of course, a longing that the
painful circumstances be changed, and this is expressed in prayers of
petition. Usually in such prayers there is some kind of reference to the
past as a basis for confidence in presenting the petition.

Psalm 80 addresses God as "the one enthroned above the cherubs"
above the ark (cf. Ex. 25:22). This is particularly fitting in a time of
national humiliation, since the ark once preceded Israel into battle,
expressing visibly their conviction that God was with them (cf. Num.
10:33–36; 1 Sam. 4). God's warlike intervention on behalf of his people
is needed now, when Israel, under the image of the vine, is defenseless
and exposed to any and every danger (vss. 12–13). God's former
interventions on behalf of the people are recalled, still using the
metaphor of the vine, as an appeal to his faithfulness and justice: how
can he now adopt a different attitude to his vine (vss. 8–13). Finally,
the psalm turns from prayer for the community to prayer for its leader
("the man at your right hand," "the son of man who has been authorized by you" vs. 17). To the Hebrew it is self-evident that the well-
being of the nation is bound up with God's blessing on their leader and
ruler. Though it would be, perhaps, of historical interest to try to
identify who precisely the psalmist had in mind—depending, of course,
on the date of writing—we could reach no certain conclusion, and the
outcome would not really contribute to our prayerful use of the psalm.
In this respect the most evident application of the psalm to our own

circumstances would be to see in it a prayer for those responsible for leadership within our own community, and, since we all belong to a number of different communities in our complex world (religious, civil, voluntary organizations, etc.) we can apply it wherever the circumstances foreseen by the psalm seem most evidently paralleled in our own experience.

Psalms 60 and 108 are so similar as to appear as two different editions of the same prayer. Psalm 60 is the simpler and, therefore, presumably the earlier version. It begins with a description of the present circumstances, interspersed with short petitions for deliverance (vss. 1, 4–5). God's promises are recalled: favor for the tribes of Gilead, Manasseh, Ephraim, and Judah, and victory over various enemies and conquest of various territories, all located around the eastern shores of the Dead Sea: Shechem, Succoth, Edom, and Moab. At present, however, none of this promised greatness is evident. With bitter irony, the poet urges the hated Philistines to exult at the sorry state in which the chosen race finds itself: "Shout 'Victory, Philistia!' " (vs. 8). He asks whether the present impotence of Israel means that God has rejected them:

> God, can you really have rejected us?
> You no longer march with our armies. (vs. 10)

The psalm concludes with a prayer for help (vss. 11–12). Again we see an interplay of past and present. The poet experiences to the full the humiliation and pain of the present moment, and looks to the past for some kind of understanding of events and confidence for the future.

The same prayer has been reworked in Psalm 108. Something of the urgency of Psalm 60 has been lost. So in Psalm 108 verses 1–6 are a prayer of thanksgiving and praise for God's greatness, his *hesed wa'emet*. The ironic invitation to the Philistines to shout victory over Israel (Ps. 60:8) has been edited out, changed to a promise that Philistia will be conquered along with Moab and Edom:

> Moab is a bowl for me to wash in
> I throw my sandal over Edom,
> and shout 'Victory!' over Philistia. (Ps. 108:9)

The reason for the reediting is probably that the original crisis to which Psalm 60 responded has passed, and Psalm 108 is not a response to any particular crisis. The introductory verse,

> My heart is ready, God,
> I mean to sing and play.
> Awake, my muse,
>   awake, lyre and harp,
> I mean to awake the Dawn! (vs. 1)

suggests that the psalm is a routine morning prayer, and the "crisis" for which it prays for help is nothing more than the routine challenge of each new day.

Psalm 83 is a vivid prayer, expressing something akin to panic: God is silent and seemingly unaware of ominous stirrings of Israel's enemies:

> God, do not remain silent,
> do not be unmoved, God, or unresponsive!
> See how your enemies are stirring,
> See how those who hate you rear their heads!
>   (vss. 1–2)

The psalmist hopes that God's past intervention on behalf of his people will be renewed. The examples of past intervention to which he appeals (vss. 9–12) are taken from the book of Judges. He is not content that Israel be saved, but asks that the enemies be punished (vss. 13–18). Given the circumstances, the prayer is not unduly vindictive. The poetic images all express, in one way or another, that the threatening armies be scattered, as tumbleweed or chaff is scattered by the wind.

Psalm 85 opens with an expression of confidence that God is savior of his people (vss. 1–3). This sounds like a rather formal act of faith, since verses 4–7 plead for a demonstration of those very qualities that verses 1–3 sounded so confident about

> Bring us back, God our savior,
> put away your indignation against us.
> Do you mean to be angry with us forever,
> to prolong your wrath from age to age?

As well as anguished petition, the psalm also expresses readiness to be quiet and wait for a response (vs. 8a). Although this is rarely expressed in the psalms, it is an essential part of authentic prayer. In this case, God's response makes the petitioner aware of his own responsibility. God is and always will be a God of *ḥesed wa'emet* (vss. 10–13), a just God who is true to himself. The effectiveness of these divine attributes is being blocked by some attitude of the people, which must be renounced before God's ever-available help can be effective:

> What God is saying means peace,
> for his people, for his friends,
> if only they renounce their folly;
> for those who fear him, his saving help is near,
> and the glory will then live in our country.
>
> (vss. 8–9)

We have already seen hints of this in Psalm 66, verse 18, and it will reappear in psalms of repentance: While help comes only from God, there is a degree of human responsibility, since our freely chosen attitudes can themselves block God's saving activity. Psalm 85 suggests that the real effectiveness of any prayer of petition lies not in any change it may produce in God, but in the change that it should effect in the petitioner.

In contrast, Psalm 79 shows no sign of recognizing any personal responsibility for present disaster, which seems to be the sack of Jerusalem in 587 B.C. The event is described in vivid detail (vss. 1–4), and recognized as God's doing, the expression of his anger:

> How much longer will you be angry, Yahweh?
> Forever?
> Is your jealously to go on smouldering like a fire?
>
> (vs. 5)

Perhaps rather illogically, the poet prays that God may take vengeance on the pagans who may be instruments of his wrath, but are in fact learning to despise the God of Israel (vss. 6–7, 10, 12–13). But the psalmist also presumes that the disaster has somehow been brought on by the sins of former generations: "Do not hold our ancestors' crimes against us . . ." (vs. 8).

The feeling that the then generation was being punished for an accumulation of the offenses of past generations seems to have been widespread at the time of the exile. It is taken for granted in Lamentations 5:7. Ezekiel takes issue with it in chapter 18, insisting that each person bears responsibility for his or her own sins and for no one else's. Ezekiel 18 is often hailed as the dawn of a sense of personal responsibility in Hebrew thought, and contrasted with a previous mentality that thought of the individual as sharing in the responsibility of the tribe or nation. It is not completely just to charge that primitive Hebrew thought could not distinguish the responsibility of the individual from the responsibility of the group to which he belonged; Genesis 19 is a story written long before Ezekiel where individuals take personal responsibility for their own fate. Nor is it true that a sense of corporate responsibility is simply a primitive stage of Israel's thought, which had to be transcended and can now be simply ignored. We are caught in the consequences of our parents' sins, though we must also take personal responsibility for acquiescing in them. We are caught in structures that perpetuate sinful patterns and, although we must admit our personal share of responsibility for them, we also need to pray, as Psalm 85 does, to be delivered from the sinfulness bequeathed to us. We are the willing victims of the sinfulness that past generations have built up, and so we become contributors to the sinful heritage that we, in turn, pass on to coming generations.

Sometimes the psalmist was so imbued with confidence in God and his willingness to save that, although the circumstances of the prayer are painful or frightening, the psalm sounds more like a hymn of praise than a lament. Psalm 115 is an example of this kind of prayer. Only in verses 1–2 is it evident that the psalmist is living among pagans who need to be brought to see the glory of Israel's God:

> Not to us, Lord, not to us,
> but to your name give the glory.
> Why should the pagans say
> "Where is your God?"

Any pain or anguish is soon swamped by pride in Yahweh, whose power is contrasted with the impotence of pagan idols (vss. 2–7). The psalm ends with a call to God's people to praise him and have confidence in him (vss. 8–13), a blessing that calls God's favor down on the people (vss. 14–16), and an enigmatic statement that the dead cannot praise Yahweh but we, the living, can (vss. 17–18). In fact most of the Old

Testament presumes that the period between birth and death is the "life" allotted to man; after death man survives in Sheol, but this is a shadowy and diminished kind of existence. But why does the psalmist suddenly allude to the very limited human life span? Presumably the implications are that the living must make use of the span allotted them; only the living can manifest the greatness of Israel's God. Human beings have a limited time at their disposal, and need to make the most of the present moment.

Psalm 144 is also a plea for salvation (vss. 12–15) when enemies threaten (vs. 11). Yet the overriding impression is joyful. The prayer begins by thanking God for the power he gives (vss. 1–2). Then, rather like Psalm 115, it alludes to human insignificance:

> Man is like a breath,
> his days are like a passing shadow. (vs. 4)

Here the thought of man's fragility and brief span of life motivates turning to God and looking to him for salvation. His coming is in the form of a thunderstorm (vss. 5–8) and, although the psalmist is aware that he hardly deserves God's attention (vs. 3) he has a "new song" to celebrate the expected intervention all ready for singing (vs. 9). Verse 11 indicates that the subject of the prayer could be the king; however, it is not a prayer for his personal glorification alone. He identifies with his people; their destiny is his and favors granted him are for their benefit.

We have already touched on a number of psalms where, in contrast to the confidence, almost exultation, of Psalms 115 and 144, the psalmist's distress is acute, and threatens even his understanding of his past experience and his knowledge of God.

Psalm 44 is the prayer of a person painfully aware of the misery of his situation and unable to understand why it should be happening. The memory of past glories (vss. 1–8) is mocked by the misery of the present (vss. 9–14). The historical background of the time of writing, which I have already sketched, helps us understand the psalmist's experience. To identify with it, so that it becomes something more than a historical curiosity, we need to be in touch with our own experiences of disillusionment.

Psalms 74, 77, and 89 are similar prayers of complete disorientation, though the precise cause of anguish is in each case slightly different. In Psalm 74 the psalmist is distressed at the destruction of the temple, which can only mean to him that God has abandoned his people (vs. 1). The psalmist feels lost on a boundless sea of misery, without sign-posts:

> deprived of signs, with no prophets left,
> who can tell us how long this will last? (vs. 9)

The psalmist in Psalm 77 suffers depression and sleeplessness, and his recall of the past only reminds him of how disastrously things have changed: "the power of the most High is no longer what it was" (vs. 10), though he can do no more than return to the recitation of the great deeds of the past (vss. 13–20). Psalm 89 is concerned with the humiliation of the king and monarchy at the time of the exile, and is again remarkable for the fearless clarity with which the psalmist contrasts God's promises to David (vss. 19–37) with present circumstances (vss. 38–45). He pleads to be allowed to see his hope vindicated before he dies; vindication must be soon (vss. 47–48).

We who live in a world marked by "future shock" should not find it difficult to identify with Psalms 44, 77, 79, and 89. We have seen many social structures change out of all recognition, and constantly find that our assumptions are called into question. If we consider ourselves liberal—"with it"—our self-images will include an ability to welcome change and impatience with the static view of the universe that canonizes the status quo. But few of us, is any, are born liberal. Children and adolescents are conservative by nature, prone to identify the world of their comparatively narrow experience with the way things are. We escape from this state only by seeing our idols destroyed, by discovering that our heroes have feet of clay, and feeling the pillars of our private universe come down around our ears. Even if we have successfully negotiated the shoals of these experiences and arrived at a certain peace with, or even joy in, the fact that the future is full of the unexpected, we are never altogether immune from losing our bearings. The most laid-back person can be shocked out of his or her sophistication and be prompted to exclaim, "Oh my God, surely not *that!*" This is the kind of experience out of which these psalms are prayed.

Prayer in personal affliction

Given the way the Israelite identified himself with his people, and the Old Testament habit of considering the people one person, it is sometimes hard to draw a sharp line between "personal" and "national" affliction. In Psalms 44, 77, 79, and 89 the circumstance of the prayer was national disaster, but it was felt so strongly and personally by the psalmist that it became a personal crisis. Other psalms sound for the most part like personal laments expressing private griefs, only to include some expressions that make one wonder whether the "person" praying has not been really the nation all along.

For example, Psalms 9–10 for the most part seem to be prayers of the oppressed for protection against their oppressors. They were originally one single psalm, as is shown by the Hebraic alphabetical structure running from the beginning of Psalm 9 to the end of Psalm. At times this has a very individual ring. In verse 13 the poet prays for deliverance "that in the gates of the daughter of Zion (i.e. Jerusalem) I may recite your praises one by one, rejoicing that you have saved me." However, at other points the oppressors seem to be pagan nations, which would make one expect that the object of their oppression be the nation of Israel rather than any individual Israelite. Thus verse 15: "The nations have sunk into a pit of their own making, they are caught by the feet in the snare they set."

Whatever the case, Psalms 9–10 are very much the voice of the oppressed. In praying them we may be giving voice to our own sense of oppression (justified or not) or to the oppression of the many who do suffer it. Taking these psalms seriously as personal prayers can bring out into the open our own sense of oppression, of being victimized and put upon, and can be the beginning of a fruitful dialogue with God.

Psalm 102 initially sounds very personal—the prayer of someone being destroyed by sickness (vss. 1–5), abandoned by his fellows (vss. 6–8), and seemingly even by God (vss. 9–11). The moments of remission experienced seem like a cruel joke:

> You picked me up only to throw me down.
> My days dwindle away like a shadow,
> I am as dry as hay. (vss. 10–11)

The psalmist's own failing strength contrasts with the abiding power of Yahweh:

> Whereas you, Yahweh, you remain forever.
> Each generation in turn remembers you.
>   (vs. 12; cf. vss. 25–27)

The contrast between the personal (vss. 1–12) and the national (vss. 13–22) sections of the psalm is so marked that one suspects that originally they were independently written, and only later combined into one prayer. Even if this is so, the fact that they have been combined illustrates how easily the psalmist's thought moved from his own personal distress to the needs of the people. Perhaps it is meant to suggest that his personal distress is compounded by the sorry state of his people.

Psalm 22 is probably the best-known example of prayer in desolation. I have already pointed out how the psalmist at first alternates between entering fully into his present distress and seeking refuge in memory of God's former benefits. His sense of abandonment by God is occasioned by sickness:

> I am like water draining away,
> my bones are all disjointed,
> my heart is like wax, melting within me.
> My palate is drier than a potsherd,
> my tongue is stuck to my jaw . . .
> I can count every one of my bones. (vss. 14–15)

This is a vivid description of the discomfort of a high fever, and the psalmist has become so emaciated he can count his bones. In addition he is surrounded by enemies, variously described as "bulls of Bashan" (an area noted for its dairy cattle), lions and dogs (vss. 12, 13, 16, 20, 21). After a plea for healing and salvation (vss. 19–20) he experiences that dawning of confidence that is not infrequent after one has poured out one's sense of desolation, and begins to look forward to thanking God publicly by a sacrifice of praise: "I shall praise you in full assembly" (vss. 22–23). The psalmist counts himself very much among the poor, and his awareness of his poverty is the basis of his confidence that God has heard him:

For he has not despised nor disdained
the poor man in his poverty,
he has not hidden his face,
but answered him when he called. (vss. 23–24)

The poor will join in the rejoicing of the thanksgiving sacrifice with
him: "The poor shall have as much as they want to eat" (vs. 26).

Psalm 28 does not describe in detail the situation out of which he
is praying, but the psalmist does beg that he may not be swept away
in the destruction of the wicked, those who are "blind to the works
of Yahweh" (vs. 5). He seems to be experiencing a sense of fright at
being entangled in a situation he sees as sinful and doomed to
destruction:

If you are silent, I shall go down to the Pit like the rest. (vs. 2)

Caught in a situation fraught with a danger he alone seems aware of,
the psalmist expresses not only fear but anger and frustration at the
wicked whose fate he fears he will share, and asks that they be repaid
for their deeds (vs. 4). There is a remarkable transition from anxiety
(vss. 1–5) to peace and joyous thanksgiving (vss. 6–9).

The poet of Psalm 31 is mainly concerned with being saved from
enemies (vss. 4, 11–13, 15), though sickness is also hinted at. In his
distress he "commits his spirit" to God (vs. 4); the life-giving breath
on which he has such a precarious hold he commits to God for safe-
keeping.

Grief, he says, "wastes away my eye, my throat, and my inmost
parts" (vs. 9, cf. also Ps. 6:7). This strange phrase reflects the way the
Hebrews imagined weeping occurred. Ever ruthlessly phenomenological, they imagined that the mechanism of weeping corresponded
exactly to their experience of emotions giving rise to tears. Deeply felt
emotion, which eventually causes us to weep, seems to well up from
deep within. It is often manifested in a disturbance felt in the lower
abdomen. We should describe it, equally unscientifically, as the stomach turning over, or having a knot in one's stomach. Another part of
the process is a constriction of the throat muscles, which we describe
as a "lump in the throat." These phenomena led the Hebrews to
believe that tears originated deep down in the intestines, were forced
up through the throat, and eventually found outlet at the eyes, bring-

ing with them part of the vital moisture of the body. Weeping, a person quite literally "poured out his or her heart," or, more graphically still, "poured out the liver." Lamentations 2:11 describes the poet weeping bitterly at the plight of his people:

> My eyes are wasted with weeping,
> my entrails shuddered,
> my liver spilled on the ground
> at the ruin of the daughters of my people.

The author of Psalm 31 feels that he has wept himself dry; he is wrung out by emotion and has poured something of his vitality out with his tears.

In Psalm 86, petition alternates with confession of God's greatness:

> Petition vss. 1–6
> Confession of God's greatness (vss. 7–10)
> Petition to be shown the way (vs. 11)
> Confession of God's greatness (vss. 12–13)
> Petition for help (vss. 14–17).

It is, then, symmetrical in its structure, and the central point is the petition for guidance in adversity:

> Lord, teach me your way,
> how to walk beside you faithfully,
> make me single-hearted in fearing your name. (vs. 11)

The psalmist seeks solution for his distress not so much in something changing the circumstances in which he finds himself as in changing himself. It is this inner change in himself that will eventually confound his enemies (vs. 17).

By contrast, Psalm 88 is a very bleak prayer, giving expression to a state of depression in which few rays of hope penetrate. The psalmist seems to himself to be experiencing a living death. Already, still alive, he is plunged into the dreary emptiness of Sheol:

> My soul is all troubled,
> my life is on the brink of Sheol.
> I am numbered among those who go down to the Pit,
> a man bereft of strength,
> a man alone among the dead . . .

> among those who have been forgotten,
> those deprived of your protecting hand. (vss. 3–5).

The psalmist feels that God has turned against him; this is his work:

> You have plunged me to the bottom of the Pit . . .
> You have turned my friends against me.
>
> (vss. 6, 8)

Hence he feels trapped: he is "in prison and unable to escape" (vs. 9), and knows the weariness of utter hopelessness and weeping; "my eyes are worn out with suffering" (vs. 9).

> Wretched, slowly dying since my youth,
> I bore your trials, I am exhausted. (vs. 15)

The psalm expresses very little hope. The psalmist says that he is not yet dead, and therefore is still open to receive God's help (vss. 11–13), but he feels that God is rejecting his prayer, and his final words are "darkness is my one companion left" (vs. 18). Not for this psalmist the sudden turn-around of emotion that we have seen in other prayers of desolation. He ends his prayer as desolate as he began. Evidently this is not his last word; there will be some development in his life. But Psalm 88 faithfully expresses a real prayer experience where no resolution of suffering appears.

Psalm 69 is a prayer in disaster which the psalmist experiences as water reaching up to his very neck (his "*nephesh*" vs. 1). We have had other occasion to note how the "waters" carry threatening overtones for the Hebrew mind; this psalm reminds us of times when we have known the threat of "waters"—the fear of being out of our depth, of being overwhelmed and swept out of control by a force much stronger than ourself. The psalmist accepts a degree of responsibility for the trouble in which he finds himself (vs. 5). His most vivid complaints are about enemies, whom he curses in verses 22–28. Like the author of Psalm 22, the psalmist ranks himself among the "lowly" and his being saved will give strength and courage to others who, like him, are "humble" (vs. 32).

In verses 35–36 there is a sudden and unexpected switch to a national perspective, expressing hope that God will save Zion and the countryside of Judah. Up to this point it is hard to imagine that the psalm is a national prayer. How can the nation be scorned and abandoned by members of its own family (vss. 7–8), or long for sympathy and find none in the pathetic words of verses 19–20? One gets the impression that any prayer can be turned into an expression of national need.

Psalms 13, 70, 120, 123, 142, and 143 are short and fairly routine prayers for deliverance.

The 71st Psalm is the poignant prayer of an aged person. Like so many other prayers of desolation, the psalm begs for protection from enemies. Declining powers leave the aged particularly vulnerable to anyone who would exploit them, and force them to be dependent on others in a way which they may find personally humiliating, and may create difficulties in relationships with others. Finally, they are deprived of the companionship of their contemporaries. Yet the aged have a wealth of memories to draw on:

> For you alone are my hope, Lord,
> Yahweh, I have trusted you since my youth,
> I have relied on you since I was born,
> You have been my portion since my mother's womb,
> and the constant theme of my praise. (vs. 4–6)

The poet sees himself as a sign of contradiction:

> to many I have seemed an enigma,
> but you are my firm refuge. (vs. 7)

He prays for a continuation of God's protection and support in old age, and hopes that he will be able to share his knowledge of the goodness of God with the coming generation (vs. 18).

Psalm 141 prays against enemies, but not in the usual way. The psalmist does not ask to be protected from the attacks of enemies, but to be strengthened against the blandishments of the wicked (vss. 3–5). He would, he claims, prefer to be ill treated by good people than treated with honor by the wicked:

> Let a good man strike or rebuke me; it is kindness,
> but let the oil of the wicked never anoint my head.
>   (vs. 5)

Trust in desolation

It is, as we have seen, not uncommon for feelings of trust to be expressed in prayers that also express great distress; in fact, there is a tendency for prayerful expression of distress to lead to a sense of confidence. However, there are some psalms where the expression of trust and praise of God stamps out any keen sense of desolation.

Thus in Psalm 3 the adversity being experienced ("More and more are turning against me, more and more rebelling against me, more and more saying about me, 'There is no help for him in God' "—vss. 1–2) is the occasion of a triumphant proclamation of trust. The painful circumstances of the prayer simply give greater force to the peaceful trust:

> Now I can lie down and go to sleep,
> and then awake, for Yahweh has hold of me.
> No fear now of those tens of thousands
> posted against me wherever I turn. (vss. 5–6)

Psalm 5 can also be classified as prayer in desolation or threat, but the danger does not sound as though it is acute. As in Psalm 86, the central petition is to know the way of God so as not to be misled by the wicked. This is an ever-present concern, rather than a pressing special need. The prayer is therefore in a low key, without high drama.

Psalm 25 is prayed in circumstances that are painful:

> Relieve the distress of my heart,
> free me from my sufferings,
> see my misery and pain,
> forgive all my sins! (vss. 17–18)

However, the prayer does not dwell much on the sufferings that prompted it; it is more concerned with the praises of God and trust in God's goodness. In verses 4–5 the psalmist prays that God may reveal his way to him. The fact that God reveals his way then becomes one of the motives of praise (vss. 8–14). It is difficult to find much development in the psalm. The themes mentioned recur in a way that seems rather jumbled, and this may have been dictated by the alphabetical form, which tends to tax the poet's ingenuity by requiring the verses to begin with successive letters of the alphabet and so take precedence over logical progression.

Psalm 4 is a prayer of petition, opening with the plea "Answer me when I call" (vs. 1). But the memory of God's goodness immediately supervenes ("You give me room when I am in trouble") and it is this note of trust that dominates the psalm. Verses 2–4 exhort the hearers to open their hearts to God, and so discover that he is the course of happiness (vs. 5). Verses 7–8 are an expression of the joy the poet finds in God.

Psalm 11 is prayed in threatening circumstances:

> See how the wicked are bending their bows
> and fitting their arrows to the string,
> ready to shoot the upright from the shadows.
> When foundations fall to ruin,
> what can the just man do? (vss. 2–3)

Though one might be tempted to fly from the threat, this is not really an option for the psalmist, who is so deeply rooted in trust:

> I have taken shelter in the Lord.
> How can you say to my soul,
> "Fly like a bird to the mountains." (vs. 1)

The psalm therefore merges into a hymn of praise of God who will see justice triumph (vss. 3–7).

Despite an initial plea, "Look after me, God, I take refuge in you" (vs. 1), Psalm 16, too, is more a cry of joy in Yahweh (vss. 4–11) than a prayer of desolation.

From confidence to distress!

At first, Psalm 27 sounds more like a song of praise than a prayer of distress. The menace of evil men cannot touch the psalmist (vs. 2); rather than pray for help, he is inclined to rejoice that it is present:

> And now my head is held high
> over the enemies who surround me.
> In his tent I will offer an exultant sacrifice.
>
> (vss. 6)

It is only later that he appears distressed:

Yahweh, hear my voice as I cry!
Pity me! Answer me!
My heart has said of you, "Seek his face."
Yahweh, I do seek your face,
hide not your face from me.
Do not repulse your servant in anger,
you are my help. (vss. 7–9)

It is as though the very keenness of the poet's appreciation of God's sustaining presence arouses a fear of losing it, although this fear does not altogether stamp out the sense of joy and confidence, and the psalm ends on a note of confidence:

This I believe,
I shall see the goodness of Yahweh in the
    land of the living.
Put your hope in Yahweh, be strong,
let your heart be bold,
put your hope in Yahweh. (vss. 13–14)

Psalm 40 expresses such a sudden and complete change of mood that it is hard to find a plausible explanation. Verses 1–10 are an ecstatic hymn of praise, prompted by a particular experience of Yahweh's help. Verses 11–17 turn to anguished pleas for help. Thanksgiving, even for so resounding a sign of God's love as verses 1–3 suggest, can lead to a new realization of a multitude of troubles remaining:

. . . for evils encompass me without number,
my iniquities have overtaken me until I cannot see.
They are more than the hairs on my head.
My heart fails me. (vss. 11–12)

Coming to terms with the human condition

I suggested earlier that the "fear of Yahweh" praised in the 10th Verse of Psalm 111 as the height of wisdom is an acceptance of God and his lordship. This acceptance has wide-reaching implications, and involves a sort of reconciliation with reality. It is not quite the same thing as canonizing the *status quo*. The *status quo* is infected by human sinfulness. Genesis 1–11 drives home again and again that, while God's activity is creative, human sinfulness is a kind of "anti-creation" and is destructive of the order and goodness of things. God's action always tends toward "re-creation"—movement toward that ideal perfection which human sinfulness prevents from being a reality. Since no human person has experienced the "ideal" state of things, descriptions of it always involve an element of imagination and conjecture.

Recognizing God's lordship, then, involves faith in the basic goodness of things. Furthermore, the Old Testament recognizes the present order of things, marred as it is by human sinfulness, as sanctioned by God. Certain features of the world as we know it are seen as the consequence of sin sanctioned by God as punishment even though they are to be superseded. Logically, then, it is a godlike task to work and act so as to remove the consequences of sin in the world; yet to do so with an underlying acceptance of those very consequences of sin, ordained and approved as they are by God. The status quo is to be accepted, though not as unchangeable, still less as ideal.

Psalm 75 is an expression of satisfaction in the basic goodness of reality, and an act of faith in the ultimate triumph of this goodness over all that remains to be superseded. But there are a number of psalms that have been inspired by the anguish resulting when this optimism is obscured—as it inevitably is at times. Most people at some time or other will be confronted by the question, "Is there justice in the world?" This question expresses a basic unease with the way things are, and it could be phrased in a number of different ways: "Is there a loving God?", "Does God care?", "Is life worth living?"

These questions presented themselves with peculiar force to people of Old Testament times. Recalling the image of man that underlies the thinking of the Old Testament, we must be struck by the fact that, in contrast with the usual Christian insistence that man possesses a spiritual and immortal soul, there is nothing in it that seems destined to last. Take away the human person's breath, and even before other signs of disintegration begin to manifest themselves, he or she is crucially different from a living person. And that is only the beginning. Very shortly the blood somehow disappears, the flesh disintegrates, and we are left with bones, a mere skeleton of the person we once were. To the question, "Are human beings mortal?", the most obvious Hebrew answer would be "Yes, dreadfully so." Not that they conceived of death as annihilation; after all, a good deal of the person manifestly survives the moment of death; but what remains is a shadow of the former self. The body is, according to Hebrew custom, buried, and returns to the dust from which it came (cf. Gen. 3:19; Eccles. 12:6–7). The human being survives after death, but it is a survival that does not deserve the name "life." He or she goes down to "Sheol," located deep in the earth, and described in terms that recall a grave. Sometimes, in fact, it is simply called "the grave," "the dust," "the earth," or "the Pit."

This picture of man and his destiny is not really a doctrine professedly taught in the Old Testament. It did not have to be taught; it was part of the mental picture of the way things were common to most peoples of the region. Old Testament revelation is basically concerned with God, who is a God of generosity and faithfulness. Given the assumptions about man just expounded, the only space in which God could be imagined exercising his generosity and faithfulness was in the earthly life of a person, the only life the Hebrews imagined was at anyone's disposal.

Isaiah 38 describes King Hezekiah thanking God for delivering him from an illness that had threatened to carry him off in the prime of life. Throughout he assumes that death would have meant the end of everything worthy of the name of life:

> I said, in the noon of my life I have to depart
>   for the gates of Sheol.
> I am deprived of the rest of my years.
> I said,
> I shall never see Yahweh again in the land
>   of the living,
> never again look on any man of those who
>   inhabit the earth . . .
> Sheol does not praise you,
> death does not extol you,
> those who go down to the Pit do not hope in
>   your faithfulness. (vss. 10–11, 18)

Hence conventional wisdom enshrined in most of the Old Testament supposes that God will show his generosity by granting blessings that can be enjoyed in the here and now: long life, abundance of riches, children who will save one's memory from complete oblivion. The wicked man, by cutting himself off from God, cut himself off from God's blessings, too, and so could look forward only to a life that was "nasty, brutish, and short." This conviction is reflected in Psalm 36. After describing the blindness of the wicked, who feel they can live without God (vss. 1–4), the psalmist hymns the generosity and faithfulness of God:

> Your love (*ḥesed*) Yahweh, reaches to the skies,
> your faithfulness (*'emunah*) to the clouds . . .
> Yes, with you is the fountain of life,
> and in your light we see light. (vss. 5, 9)

The ultimate disaster that could befall a sinner was deprivation of material goods and health, and to see his children wiped out, thus robbing him of any kind of immortality. The severest curse of Psalm 109 against enemies is:

> May his family die out,
> its name disappear in one generation. (vs. 13)

One has to be blind to many facts of observation seriously to maintain that the good necessarily prosper and live long, contented lives, and that the evil die young after a life of suffering. So this kind of simplistic optimism is very susceptible to crisis, and throughout the Old Testament we see people struggling to bring the unchanging conviction of God's goodness and fidelity into realistic confrontation with the facts of life.

Thus Psalm 53 reflects on the fate of the wicked, and marvels at the apparent extent of wickedness (vss. 1–4). Verse 6 seems to suggest that the historical setting is the exile, and these reflections would be prompted and sharpened by the ascendancy of pagans. However, the psalmist expresses confidence that the balance will be righted (vss. 5–6). Psalm 14 differs from it only in that it usually uses the title "Yahweh" where Psalm 53 uses "God."

Psalm 12 is a similar cry of fear and distress at wickedness rampant:

> There are no devout men left,
> fidelity has vanished from mankind. (vss. 1–2)

The psalmist pleads with God to punish the wicked (vss. 3–4) and feels confidence that his prayer has been heard (vs. 5).

Psalm 94 is a longer prayer on the same theme, prompted by the arrogance and seeming ascendancy of the wicked. Verse 20 suggests that some national disaster may have prompted the prayer, since "disorder is imposed as law." The psalmist is filled with confidence, even a sense of superiority, based on his memory of God's past favors (vss. 14–19).

Psalm 58 is inspired by a particular form of wickedness: the abuse of power. Though "gods," the oppressors have not behaved as such (vss. 1–2). Hebrew does not reserve the word "god" for Yahweh. It is usual to imagine Yahweh surrounded by a heavenly court of "gods" (cf. Ps. 82:1), who can also be called "sons of God" (cf. Job. 1:6). More rarely, privileged human beings, especially those entrusted with the power to rule, are designated "gods," presumably because they are incorporated into Yahweh's "court." This is the case in Psalm 58:1 and 82:6; and in Psalm 45:6 the king seems to be called "god." In Hebrew usage, then, there are many "gods," but only one Yahweh, "exalted far above all gods."

Psalm 82 arises out of similar moral indignation over the unworthiness of the "gods" who "carry on blindly, undermining the basis of human society" (vs. 5). The psalm is mainly descriptive, picturing God pronouncing sentence on unworthy rulers. We as spectators are invited to say "Amen" to the sentence:

> Rise, God, judge the world,
> because you are great among the nations. (vs. 8)

Other psalms move beyond righteous indignation or amazement at the prevalence and seeming success of the wicked and begin to struggle with the problems about the goodness and power of God that this can raise. Psalm 37 is full of good advice for the person troubled by such questions. The psalmist urges his hearers to abandon the whole question to God. The triumph of the "wicked" is short-lived, and the "good" will eventually be vindicated. God will satisfy the questioner's "heart's desire":

> Trust in Yahweh and do what is good,
> make your home in the land and live in peace.
> Make Yahweh your only joy,
> and he will give you what your heart desires. (vss. 3–4)

> Be quiet before Yahweh and wait patiently for him . . .
> Enough of anger, leave rage aside,
> Do not worry, nothing good can come of it. (vss. 7–8)

The psalmist shows, however, a certain unwillingness to face awkward facts, claiming:

> I was young, now I am old,
> but I have never seen a virtuous man deserted,
> nor his descendants forced to beg their bread.
> He is always compassionate, always lending,
> his children will be blessed. (vss. 25–26)

One has the uneasy feeling that it had to be the conventional answer, right or wrong, even if he had to shut his eyes to facts to maintain it. Even his counsel to put aside the problem is at least not always practicable, and can probably never be a final answer.

Psalm 73 is almost at the other end of the scale, a prayer of thanksgiving after weathering a crisis of faith brought on by the question of the justice of Yahweh. The psalmist has in fact now reached a haven of peace and contentment:

> I look to no one else in heaven,
> I delight in nothing else on earth,
> my flesh and my heart are pining with love,
> my heart's rock, my own, God for ever!"
>   (vss. 25–26)

But it was not always so, and he relives his crisis of faith vividly. The psalm begins with an act of faith in God's goodness:

> How good God is to Israel,
> the Lord is good to pure hearts. (vs. 1)

But this was precisely the subject of his doubts, as he envies the proud and the arrogant, who seemed to him to have so much and to lack so little. Verse 9 is probably a rather bizarre description of the insatiably avaricious:

> They put their mouths on the heavens
> and their tongues lash to and fro on earth.

Their maw encompasses the whole of creation. Their mouths open so wide as to reach to the heavens, and their tongues lash to and fro, sweeping up the contents of the earth to be swallowed.

He finds the traditional answers to his dissatisfaction unconvincing. When suffering could not be seen as the consequence of sin, Proverbs 3:11–12 explained it as loving discipline from God:

> My son, do not scorn correction from Yahweh,
>   do not resent his rebuke.
> For Yahweh reproves the man he loves,
>   as a father checks a well-loved son.

To this kind of consideration the poet of Psalm 73 replies:

> After all, why should I keep my own heart pure,
>   and wash my hands in innocence,
> if you plague me all day long,
>   and discipline me every morning. (vss. 13–14)

This is the complaint of someone tired of pious cliches as the answer to real distress.

There is a temptation, in moments of uncertainty, to settle for one or another answer simply to escape the tension of uncertainty. The psalmist felt this temptation, but chose to live with the uncertainty and all its uncomfortable consequences. His honesty is rewarded by a flash of insight:

> Had I said, "That talk appeals to me,"
> I should have abandoned your people's race.
> Instead, I tried to analyze the problem,
>   hard though I found it,
> until the day I pierced the mystery,
>   and saw the end in store for them. (vss. 14–17)

His insight is in fact neither particularly new nor, to the observer, particularly satisfying: the prosperity of the wicked is part of their punishment, leading them on to ruin. But for the psalmist it meets his need, and he can now look back on his experience and, while criticizing his foolishness, see that his salvation lay in remaining in God's presence with all the unpleasant and unsettling emotions:

> When my heart had been growing sourer,
> with pains shooting through my loins,
> I had simply failed to understand,
> my stupid attitude to you was brutish.
> Even so, I stayed in your presence,
> you held my right hand. (vss. 21–23)

Psalm 73 provides us with something of a paradigm of crisis successfully weathered without any compromise of honesty or integrity.

Psalm 49 does not take us so deeply into the experience of the poet, but it does express a particularly profound reflection on human happiness. The psalmist has a sharp sense of the human condition being limited, finite, mortal:

> . . . man could never buy himself back,
> or pay the price of his life to God.
> It costs so much to redeem his life it is beyond him.
> How then could he live on forever
> and never see the pit,
> when all the while he sees that wise men die,
> that foolish and stupid perish both alike
> and leave their wealth to others;
> their tombs are their eternal home. . . . (vss. 7–11)

Realizing this basic and unpalatable fact about human life puts prosperity and hardship, success and failure, into a new perspective. In fact, the psalmist suggests that riches are dangerous because they blind man to the realization of his mortality:

> Man when he prospers forfeits intelligence,
> he is one with the cattle doomed to slaughter.
> So on they go in their self-assurance . . .
> (vss. 12–13)

Their passing is like the passing of a dream (vs. 14), but the psalmist has some kind of obscure faith that he will be spared this fate:

> But God will redeem my life
> from the grasp of Sheol
> and will receive me. (vs. 15)

The Christian will immediately read this as a hope of heaven, though we cannot be sure that the psalmist was thinking of something so explicit and clear. Perhaps he was content to escape the lot of those who go mindlessly to death.

A theologically correct statement about the God of Israel would define him as the God who gives life and wishes to bestow it in its fullness. Yet the reality of God is so complex, and his dealings with us so varied, that they defy categorization. And there will be times when we *feel* painful aspects of our relationship with him. Psalm 39 acknowledges and expresses rebellion against the sense of human fragility. It is perhaps all the more poignant in that this is a prayer of someone who subscribes to an almost stoic ideal of accepting suffering with resignation. Twice (vss. 1–3 and vs. 9) the psalmist expresses his resolution to keep silence, but each time the vehemence of his emotions forces him to give them expression.

> My heart had been smouldering inside me,
> and it flared up at the thought of this
>   (i.e. the prosperity of the wicked)
> and the words burst out. (vs. 3)

He prays to know his own frailty:

> Tell me, Yahweh, when my end will be,
> how many days are allowed me,
> show me how frail I am. (vs. 4)

This gives him a sense of the relative unimportance of riches: "wealth ... is only a puff of wind ..." (vs. 6). The realization does not quiet his distress; he begs for deliverance (vss. 7–8) and again resolves to be silent (vs. 9), since his suffering is the work of God and he therefore cannot question it:

> I am dumb, I speak no more,
> since you yourself have been at work. (vs. 9)

Again he cannot keep silent, and dares to pray that God will leave him alone:

> Lay your scourge aside,
> I am worn out with the blows you deal me.
> You punish man with the penalties of sin,

> like a moth you eat away all that gives him pleasure;
> man is indeed only a puff of wind. (vss. 10–11)

The psalmist, a guest in God's world, begs space to live and breathe and enjoy the little time granted him:

> I am your guest, and only for a time,
> a nomad like all my ancestors.
> Look away, that I may draw breath,
> before I go away and am no more! (vss. 12–13)

Here we are a far cry from rejoicing in God or relishing his presence. There is, certainly, a tension between the sentiments expressed in Psalm 39 and the "faith" of both the Old and the New Testaments. But our security in our faith is better indicated by the ability to acknowledge contrary sentiments than by anxious defensiveness that tries to crush such sentiments as disloyal. A faith that cannot be questioned or examined critically is a fragile faith indeed. A God who cannot allow us to express our fears and our anger is an insecure God. Our prayers to him would have to imitate the falsity of much human interaction, where we dare express only what the other person wants to hear. The psalmists knew a more robust God, with whom one could really dare to communicate.

Psalm 90 also expresses painful experience of God, but the psalm probably comes from some special period of suffering, rather than from a general sense of the difficulty of the human condition. Verses 7–8 seem to suggest that those who are praying have in some special way experienced the harsh face of God:

> We too are burnt up by your anger,
> and terrified by your fury;
> having summoned up our sins,
> you inspect our secrets by your own light. (vss. 7–8)

The psalmist hopes that this present suffering will eventually seem like a bad dream:

> Let us wake in the morning filled with your love,
> and sing and be happy all our days.
> Make our future happy as our past was sad,
> those years when you were punishing us. (vss. 14–15)

Still, whatever the precise circumstances, the author has, through them, become aware of the underlying precariousness of human living:

> Before the mountains were born . . .
> you were God . . .
> You can turn men back into dust . . .
> You brush men away like waking dreams,
> they are like grass, sprouting and flowering
> in the morning,
> withered and dry before dusk. (vss. 2–6)
> . . . our lives are over in a breath,
> our life lasts seventy years,
> eighty for those who are strong,
> and most of these are emptiness and pain,
> they pass swiftly, and we are gone. (vss. 9–10)

Yet the author feels that somewhere in this seemingly bottomless pit of emptiness wisdom is to be found—perhaps something like the other side of the coin of fear of Yahweh:

> Teach us to count the few days we have,
> and so gain wisdom of heart. (vs. 12)

He also knows that there is another side to the experience of life and of God, and prays to be granted the experience of Yahweh's sweetness (vss. 14–17).

In Old Testament times, the persecution of faithful Jews under Antiochus IV Epiphanes, in 165 B.C., forced a radical questioning of some of the assumptions about man and his relationship with God. We saw an echo of this in Psalm 44. Far from guaranteeing long life and prosperity, faithful observance of the law could bring suffering and death. The naive optimism of Psalm 37 was discredited and some of the questions reinforced. Either one abandoned faith in Yahweh as the God of generosity and faithfulness, or one made a great leap of faith, asserting that even death itself would not prevent Yahweh from bestowing the fullness of his gifts on those whom he loves. The only way in which Hebrew thought could envisage this was by the way of resurrection—reconstituting the bodily composite that is a human being. So Daniel 12:2 could assert that of those who lay sleeping in the dust "many will awake, some to everlasting life, some to shame and everlasting disgrace." Still later, in the book of Wisdom, an author exposed to the categories of Greek thought could speak of man's immortality and continuing life after death in some disembodied state. There are no psalms that incontrovertibly incorporate these ideas.

However, the expectation of life after death is very much part of Christianity. At times one has the impression that Christians are primarily interested in the next life, so that earthly life becomes simply a time of waiting, avoiding anything that could be an obstacle to enjoying happiness in the next. Can Christians, then, in any way identify with the anguish and uncertainties of people who did not have this consoling answer to their questions about human destiny?

Christians are not immune from feeling the menace of their own mortality. By and large, we share in the unwillingness to face up to death that is endemic in modern Western society. We gloss it over with pretty phrases. We do not like to talk about deadly diseases. Suffering still *feels* like an affront, something we should not have to put up with. There are times when the God who sanctions suffering seems a harsh, cruel God, because our emotional reaction is to what we feel here and now, and our experience of the goodness of God can recede into a distant memory.

As I have insisted throughout, to deny our feelings is a dishonesty that never works. Deep down inside ourselves somewhere we know the truth and are further hurt and infuriated by our attempts to deny it. The here and now, the stuff of our experience, is the place where God reveals himself. To be caught up in living by anticipation in a world we have never seen is to run the risk of making our religion an unreal thing, a castle in the clouds.

The here and now is all we have to operate with. I believe we could claim that even Christianity is first and foremost concerned with the quality of people's lives here and now. When James and John tried to assure for themselves high places in a future glorious kingdom, Jesus directed their attention back to the demands of the present moment: "Can you drink the cup that I must drink, and be baptized with the baptism with which I must be baptized?" (Mk. 10:35–40), and disclaimed any interest in the other question, which he left in the care of his Father. It is not possible or desirable to dismiss the present moment as irrelevant; we can and should be asking ourselves if we are making the best possible use of the present moment.

Praying from a sense of sin

The Old Testament knows three ways by which a person may be brought to a sense of sin: the experience of God, a sudden vision of oneself from an objective, outsider's point of view, and the experience of desolation.

A striking example of the first of these is the experience recounted in Isaiah 6. A man imbued with a deep love of Jerusalem and its institutions, Isaiah becomes aware of his special mission in the temple in Jerusalem; it is an experience of the overwhelming power, majesty, and immensity of God:

> In the year of King Uzziah's death, I saw the Lord Yahweh
> seated on a high throne; his train filled the sanctuary; above him
> stood seraphs, each one with six wings: two to cover its face, two
> to cover its feet, and two for flying. (Is. 6:1–2)

This impression of God's majesty is summed up in the word "holy," primarily signifying the transcendence of God, that quality which inspires awe in us. It is in turn connected with the idea of "glory," which in turn is connected with the word "weighty" and perhaps could be best expressed by the English word "overwhelming."

> They cried out to each other in this way:
> "Holy, holy, holy is Yahweh Sabaoth.
> His glory fills the whole earth."
> The foundations of the threshhold shook
> with the voice of the one who cried out,
> and the Temple was filled with smoke. (vss. 3–4)

Isaiah responds to this overwhelming majesty of God with a deep sense of his own unworthiness:

> What a wretched state I am in; I am lost. For I am a man of
> unclean lips, and I live among a people of unclean lips, and my
> eyes have seen the King, Yahweh Sabaoth. (vs. 5)

This sense of sin does not arise from examination of his own conduct. It is a sudden insight into the condition of man in the light of God. It is a particularly vivid realization of the finiteness of man, for which Psalm 39:4 and Psalm 90:12 prayed, the latter with the feeling that in it is to be found wisdom. It is at first a crushing experience, as expressed in Isaiah's words just quoted. Being crushed (and "crushed" is the etymological meaning of "contrite") is a necessary step along the way to new wholeness. This is expressed in Isaiah's vision by the searing experience of being cleansed by burning coal:

> Then one of the seraphs flew to me, holding in his hand a live coal which he had taken from the altar with a pair of tongs. With this he touched my mouth and said "See now, this has touched your lips. Your sin is taken away, your iniquity purged."
> (vss. 6–7)

The end result of this humbling and cleansing process is a sense of wholeness and confidence that shows itself in Isaiah's magnanimous eagerness to do great things:

> Then I heard the voice of the Lord saying:
> "Whom shall I send? Who will be our messenger?"
> I answered, "Here I am, send me." (vss. 8–9)

Isaiah's meeting with God is a very graphic account of the experience of awe, and spells out something of what is implied in Psalm 8, where the sense of God mediated by the sight of the starry heavens evokes first a sense of insignificance in the psalmist but ultimately a sense of the worth and importance of the human person:

> I look up at the heavens, made by your fingers,
> at the moon and the stars you set in place,
> ah, what is man that you should spare a thought for him,
> the son of man that you should care for him?
> Yet you have made him little less than a god,
> You have crowned him with glory and splendor....
> (Ps. 8:3–5)

The second way of becoming aware of one's sinfulness, by suddenly stepping outside oneself and seeing oneself objectively, is well exemplified in David's realization of the sinfulness of his adultery with the wife of Uriah the Hittite, aggravated as it was by his engineering the death of Uriah to cover up the sin (2 Sam. 11–12).

The prophet Nathan confronts him with an account of his own behavior, thinly disguised in the form of a story of a rich man who had an abundance of sheep at his disposal yet chooses to steal the one and only sheep of a poor man. David is detached enough from this situation to see the wickedness involved and become indignant at it:

> David's anger flared up against the man. "As Yahweh lives," he said to Nathan, "the man who did this deserves to die! He must make fourfold restitution for the lamb, for doing such a thing and not showing compassion." Then Nathan said to David, "You are the man . . ." (2 Sam. 12:5–7). David said to Nathan, "I have sinned against Yahweh.'" (2 Sam. 12:13)

In this particular instance, the effectiveness of the process is furthered by tricking the sinner into distancing himself from his action, so that he sees it with new objectivity. Much of the preaching of the prophets serves this purpose, though not always to such effect: they present the people with an objective view of their conduct.

Psalm 50 is one psalm that aims at fulfilling this kind of purpose. Perhaps significantly, it is placed immediately before Psalm 51, the most famous of the psalms of repentant prayer. It is also cast in the form of God's Word to his people. Usually the psalms express the other side of the dialogue which is prayer: human words to God. If prayer is to be effective, the person praying must also be ready to leave space for the other side of the dialogue: God's Word spoken in his or her heart. Though Psalm 51 is God's Word to the person praying, there must still be space left for the human response to the word of God.

The relationship between God and his people is often described in the Old Testament in terms of the relationship between a great king and his vassals. The terms governing such relationships were contained in treaties or covenants between the great king and the vassal peoples, which normally followed a stereotyped pattern. The Ten Commandments, the laws of the book of Deuteronomy, and the "Code of Holiness" (Lev. 17–26) all follow more or less closely the pattern of these treaties, with God in the role of the great king, his people in the role of a conquered nation. Psalm 50 also makes use of this image, describing God's lawsuit against his people, accusing them of having been unfaithful to the covenant. It begins with a grandiose description of Yahweh coming to judge and summoning witnesses to the trial. In secular treaties between pagan nations the witnesses were normally the gods of the respective nations. In the covenant between God and Israel it is traditionally "heaven and earth" that function as witnesses to the covenant. Drawing on the common image of God's approach, the psalm describes him coming in a thunderstorm:

> Yahweh, God of gods, speaks.
> He summons the earth.
> From east to west, from Zion, perfection of beauty,
>   he shines . . .
> Before him, devouring fire, round him a raging storm,
> he summons the heavens above, and the earth,
> to his people's trial. (vss. 1–4)

The substance of the complaint is one familiar to most of the earlier prophets. Ritual sacrifice can easily become, in the minds of the devotees, something that God needs to keep him happy, instead of something that human beings need to express their deep sense of dependence on and dedication to God. Religious practices can easily become ways of controlling God and bending him to our will rather than a way of totally submitting ourselves to him. Psalm 50 aims at righting the perspective; sacrifice is not something that God needs (vss. 8–13). Thankfulness is a pleasing offering to him (vs. 14). Finally the psalm challenges the person who can recite the terms of the covenant between God and his people, but who overlooks the glaring inconsistencies in his own life (vss. 15–23), and verse 23 returns again to thankfulness as a disposition of basic importance.

Psalm 81 begins with a shout of triumph and joy in God (vss. 1–5), but the rest of the psalm is put into God's mouth: a recitation of his great deeds on behalf of the people (vss. 6–7), an appeal to the people for loyalty and fidelity (vss. 8–10) and reproach for infidelity (vss. 11–16). Verse 16 expresses God's desire to shower benefits on his people, which is the basis of his desire to have us live his way:

> If only my people would listen,
> if Israel would follow my ways. . . .
> I would feed you on finest wheat,
> and satisfy you with wild rock honey. (vss. 12–16)

This is not just a reward attached to obedience. The person who refuses to accept God disqualifies himself or herself from really knowing happiness.

In Psalm 15 both sides of the divine-human dialogue are represented, verse 1 seeking direction from God, and the rest of the psalm being God's response:

> Yahweh, who has the right to enter your tent,
> or to live on your holy mountain? (vs. 1)

God's response centers on a demand for integrity: "speaking the truth from the heart (vs. 2), standing by one's pledge (vs. 4), and right relations with one's fellows—avoiding slander—(vs. 3), "not doing evil to one's neighbor" (vs. 3), not lending money for interest—implying a readiness to lend without interest (vs. 4), and not accepting bribes (vs. 5). This is a necessarily inadequate expression of man's seeking and God's response; the manner in which God "teaches his way" to those who seek him can hardly be adequately expressed in words.

Psalm 15 recalls Psalm 24:3–4 where, in response to the question "Who has the right to climb the mountain of Yahweh, who the right to stand in his holy place?", certain other requirements are enunciated. Some scholars have conjectured that these psalms reflect a practice of greeting those seeking entrance to the temple with a recital of such requirements. Some go further still, speculating that the Ten Commandments were composed for use in this ceremonial setting. Neither conjecture is very convincing, and the latter overlooks that the commandments are in the form of commands, while these psalms are in the form of statements of what God requires of those who seek him.

Psalm 82 is somewhat similar, being a divine challenge to the rather specialized group who abuse positions of power.

If psalms of this nature become the living Word of God to us, we will experience them as a two-edged sword, piercing through the armor of routine and unawareness with which we normally ward off threats to our complacency. We will experience them as a revelation of the hollowness of our own living (in the case of Ps. 50 or Ps. 81) or as a very personal challenge to ourselves (in the case of Ps. 15). However, even if they only provoke reactions of boredom or even annoyance at their very triteness, it reveals to us something of ourselves. It may reveal how limited is our readiness to accept any challenge to the self-chosen tenor of our existence. It may reveal an anxiety about the quality of life that we mask by impatience at the very suggestion of challenge. In fact, the more vehement our rejection

that these psalms may have much revelance for us, the more likely it
is that we are defending part of ourselves we instinctively know
cannot bear scrutiny in the light of God.

A third way in which the Scriptures envisage a person becoming
aware of his or her sinfulness is through the experience of desolation
and suffering. Psalm 32 describes this process vividly. The psalmist
looks back on his own experience of being caught in suffering; until
he recognizes his sinfulness, he feels he is being eaten away from
within:

> All the time I kept silent,
> my bones were wasting away with groans,
> day in and day out.
> Day and night your hand lay heavy on me;
> my heart grew parched as stubble in a summer drought.
>
> (vss. 3–4)

The crucial step, allowing the healing power of God to go to work,
is acknowledgment of sin:

> At last I admitted to you that I had sinned,
> no longer concealing my guilt;
> I said,
> "I will go to Yahweh and confess my fault"
> And you, you have forgiven the wrong I did,
> have pardoned my sin. (vss. 4–5)

The destructive force of sin can be healed only when we accept our
responsibility for it. We fight against the pain and distress of sin by
refusing to acknowledge the justice of it; once we have ceased to fight
it an all-important shift has occurred. We are no longer like a dumb
animal that fights against the goad; we allow ourselves to be led:

> Do not be like senseless horse or mule
> that need bit and bridle to curb their spirit
> else they will not approach you.
> Many torments await the wicked
> but grace enfolds the man who trusts in Yahweh.
>
> (vss. 9–10)

This suggests an experience of hardness and tension in any person
fighting against God's action to move him or her to acknowledge his

or her sin. To go along with God's action involves a willingness to be broken, to be stripped of one's self-sufficiency, a real dying in order to live. The solution does not lie in discovering a new way of coping with the pain and distress one is experiencing, but in acknowledging that one cannot deal with it successfully; it is a reality for which there is no answer, and we must allow ourselves to be carried along by it without struggling against it.

Psalm 38 also includes acknowledgment of responsibility for sufferings, a combination of sickness (vss. 3–8), abandonment by friends (vs. 11), and attack by enemies (vs. 12). The attacks of enemies leave the psalmist unmoved:

> I am like the deaf, I do not hear,
> like the dumb man who does not open his mouth;
> I am like the man who, hearing nothing,
> gives no sharp answer in return,
> for I put my trust in you, Yahweh. . . . (vss. 15–16)

The very inevitability and inescapability of his distress brings him to acknowledge his own responsibility for it:

> And now my fall is upon me,
> there is no relief for my pains,
> yes, I admit my guilt,
> I am sorry for having sinned. (vss. 17–18)

The psalm ends with a plea for release from suffering, but does not describe any sense of relief at having acknowledged guilt, as did Psalm 32.

Even Psalm 39, though very different in spirit from Psalms 32 and 38 in that the psalmist never seems to become reconciled to his sufferings, takes it for granted that suffering is the consequence of sin: "Free me from all my sins" (vs. 8), and "You punish man with the penalties of sin" (vs. 10).

Psalm 6 is the prayer of someone suffering sickness ("my bones are in torment, my throat (*nephesh*) in utter torment," vs. 2); the onset of enemies (vs. 7); the psalmist has wept himself dry ("my eye is wasted with grief" vs. 7). It does not elaborate at any length on his sense of sin, but takes for granted that the Lord is making his displeasure known through these sufferings:

> Yahweh, do not punish me in your anger,
> do not reprove me in the heat of your anger. (vs. 1)

The psalm ends with one of those sudden reversals of mood from distress to utter confidence that we note so often in psalms of desolation (vss. 8–10).

In Psalm 25 the poet does not elaborate on the nature of his sufferings, but assumes that they are caused by sin, and relief of the one will be linked with forgiveness of the other:

> See my misery and pain,
> forgive all my sins! (vs. 18).

He believes strongly in the sinner's need for guidance, praying that Yahweh may reveal his way to him (vs. 4), and taking comfort from Yahweh's proven readiness to show sinners the right way (vss. 8, 12, and 14). The psalm ends with the plea:

> Redeem Israel, O God,
> from all his distress. (vs. 21)

This is another example of how a psalm that sounds like a purely personal prayer can suddenly be applied to the nation as a whole.

Psalm 41 is another prayer in sickness, when the sick person's enemies are gloating over his downfall and congratulating themselves on his imminent demise. Again the psalmist accepts his sorry state as the result of sin:

> Yahweh, take pity on me,
> Cure me, for I have sinned against you. (vs. 4)

On the other hand, the person who cared for the poor and the weak will be comforted by Yahweh in his own sickness (vs. 1–3), which obviously supposes that he will not be spared the experience of illness.

To allow that suffering may be a sign of God's displeasure and so reveal our sinfulness does not come easily to moderns. We are more inclined to see suffering as an unfortunate breakdown in the mechanism of things that could have been avoided for the most part by better use of modern technology. If we feel physical distress we assume a malfunction in the machine which is our body, and look to a physician for help. Spiritual or mental distress, if extreme, will send us to a psychiatrist, looking for an adjustment to our psychic mechanism. The thought that we ourselves could be responsible does not come easily to us: suffering is inflicted from outside by malevolent forces like viruses and bacteria, or is just one of those things that happen.

Christians perhaps have added reason for not accepting responsibility for their suffering. Did not Jesus, himself the sinless one, suffer, thus showing us that suffering is somehow noble and good? If we suffer, it is a share in the sufferings of Christ, and if we are very spiritual we may manage to regard suffering even as a gift from God, a privilege.

If it is suggested that we ourselves may be responsible for much of the suffering and desolation in our lives, our reaction will probably be angry defensiveness. Our experience of life teaches us that it is better to avoid responsibility. Our life seems generally to have been at the mercy of people who could make us unhappy—our parents and teachers of our childhood, the bosses and "higherups" of our adult life—and God all through. We could escape their dominance largely by avoiding responsibility. There are other reasons that make refusal to accept responsibility for our wounded state a tempting option. It opens up to us the seductive pleasures of self-pity, of feeling persecuted, of self-righteous, self-justifying anger. But this also means that we are committed to not changing—how can we change what we have no hand in anyway? Change does not come easily. We cannot even see *how* to change some aspects of our lives. But an acknowledgment of responsibility is like the first break in a logjam—a seemingly insignificant movement that allows the mighty force of the current—which is God's grace and always present and active—to clear the whole tightly packed mass.

Modern medicine is becoming more and more inclined to recognize that much physical illness is self-inflicted. In myriads of subtle ways we choose illness as an attractive alternative to the frightening responsibilities of being fully alive. Nor does Christianity renounce the Old Testament assumption that suffering can be the consequence of sin. In the gospels generally, physical healing is considered a manifestation of a deeper healing (cf. Mk. 2:1–12). Paul considers that the disunity of the Christian community at Corinth is having discernible effects:

> This (disunity and unworthy celebration of the Eucharist) is why
> many of you are weak and ill and some of you have died. If only
> we had recollected ourselves, we should not have been punished
> like that. But when the Lord does punish us like that, it is to
> correct us and to stop us being condemned with the world. (1
> Cor. 11:31–32)

It is premature to suppose that, for the Christian, suffering and sickness never have anything to do with sin.

Some psalms complain of suffering that is quite undeserved. Psalm
7, praying for defense against enemies, dares to say:

> Yahweh, my God, if I ever
> soiled my hands with fraud,
> repaid a friend evil for good,
> spared a man who wronged me
> (against the law requiring proportionate vengeance in Ex. 21:25)
> then let the enemy hound me down and catch me. . . .
> Give judgment for me, Yahweh,
> as my virtue and integrity deserve. (vss. 3–5, 8)

Psalm 35, also praying for defense against enemies, complains that the
psalmist had had nothing but concern for the people who have now
turned against him (vss. 11–13). Psalm 59:4 also complains that the
attacks of the psalmist's enemies are unprovoked:

> For no offense, no sin of mine, Yahweh,
> how they hurry into position.

Psalm 17, also against enemies, sounds still more self-satisfied:

> You probe my heart, examine me at night,
> you test me, yet find nothing, no murmuring from me;
> my mouth has not sinned as most men's do.
> No, I have treasured the words from your lips,
> in the path prescribed, walking deliberately,
> in your footsteps so that my feet do not slip.
>
> (vss. 3–5)

Psalm 44:17–19, in the face of national suffering, laments that "this
has befallen us though we had not forgotten you. . . ."

The profession of innocence is still more prominent in Psalm 26, and there is not much description of any painful circumstances—so the prayer sounds uncomfortably like a prayer of exultation in one's own goodness. The psalmist is not content to assert his innocence, but calls upon God to scrutinize him to the depths of his being—almost defying God to discover sin in him:

> Yahweh, be my judge! . . .
> Test me, Yahweh, and probe me,
> put me to the trial, loins and heart,
> for your love is before my eyes,
> and I live my life in loyalty to you. (vss. 1–3)

The psalmist seems to have no qualms about his innocence, and is serenely confident that God's scrutiny will vindicate him. Yet in verses 9–10 some misgivings appear:

> Do not let my soul share the fate of sinners,
> or my life the doom of men of blood,
> men with guilt on their hands,
> whose right hands are heavy with bribes." (vss. 9–10)

These misgivings do not come from a sense of personal guilt. The author sees himself implicated in a sinful situation to which he is not aware of contributing, but in whose downfall he fears he may be swept away. So, despite his sense of personal innocence, he can still plead for deliverance:

> But I live my life in innocence,
> redeem me, Yahweh, take pity on me.
> My foot is set on the right path,
> I bless you, Yahweh, in the assemblies. (vss. 11–12)

Can anyone really claim such innocence? Especially, can anyone be so closely associated with sinners as to feel the danger of being swept away in their downfall and claim utter innocence? Even in the other psalms protesting innocence, all of which complain that the psalmists' enemies attack with no provocation, there may well be a certain amount of self-deception, a blindness to ways in which enemies have been unwittingly provoked or ways in which the "victim" has set himself up for victimization. These psalms express a level of consciousness that may well need to be deepened to a recognition of all sorts of subtle ways in which the individual may be responsible for what befalls him.

If we let psalms like these (Pss. 7, 17, 26) speak to our hearts we will very probably discover within ourselves barely acknowledged feelings of being unjustly treated, of not being appreciated, of not having our efforts recognized. No matter whether these feelings are justified or not, it is a joy to pour out that sense of being wronged and misjudged to God. But it is only one side of the dialogue, and we must leave room in our hearts to hear God's response. We probably also have an internal censor that tells us it is bad to have such feelings, but this is not necessarily the voice of God. It may well be the voice of experience, which warns us that expressing such feelings openly is likely to get us into deeper trouble than ever—despised for weakness and seeking sympathy. Feelings like that are best cherished in private, or at most shared with a sympathetic and supportive friend. God's response may not support us in our sense of being victimized.

The book of Job is a long dialogue on the mystery of suffering. Job, the innocent sufferer, insists on his innocence, while his friends propound various ways of "explaining" the experience of suffering. In the end God reveals himself to Job in all his power and majesty, manifested in the works of creation. Not a word of explanation is offered for his suffering, yet Job finds himself satisfied. He has not been given a logical explanation of the questions he had wrestled with, but the insight into the power and mystery of God has stilled the disquiet of which his questioning was only a symptom:

This was the answer Job gave to Yahweh:

> "I know that you are all-powerful.
>   What you conceive, you can perform.
> I am the man who obscured your designs
>   by my empty-headed words.
> I have been holding forth on matters I cannot understand,
>   on marvels beyond me and my knowledge.
> I knew you then only by hearsay,
>   but now, having seen you with my own eyes,
> I retract all I have said,
> and in dust and ashes I repent. (Job. 42:1–6).

Somehow Job could come to this new peace only by recognizing how inadequate were his friends' explanations of the mystery of suffering, and he is commended by God for "speaking honestly" about God (cf. Job. 42:7–8).

Suffering cannot be explained; it can only be experienced, though we would willingly avoid the experience if we could. The psalmists regularly find an answer to the challenge and ultimate satisfaction by entering fully into their suffering in a prayerful way. For some at least, entering into their suffering in this way leads them to recognize that they are responsible for it, and this recognition is the shift of attitude that opens the way to healing.

Psalm 130 is a prayer "from the depths," which implies an experience of the lostness and hopelessness of being a sinner. The poet recognizes that he alone cannot cope with his sin, but for him the coming of Yahweh is as certain as the dawn, longed for anxiously but never really in question.

In Psalm 143 the psalmist also recognizes that he cannot bear the full weight of his sins:

> Do not put your servant on trial,
> no one is virtuous by your standards"
> (vs. 2)

Recognizing responsibility for one's own life does not imply that one claims full control over the situation resulting from sin. The psalmist seeks comfort from the memory of God's great deeds (vss. 5–6), and begs deliverance from imminent disaster.

Psalm 51 must be the most famous prayer of penitence. In it the poet accepts full responsibility for his sin and hence acknowledges the "rightness" of God's judgment on it:

> For I am well aware of my faults,
> I have my sin constantly in mind,
> having sinned against none other than you,
> having done what you regard as wrong.
> You are just when you pass sentence on me,
> blameless when you give judgment. (vss. 3–4)

At the same time the psalmist is aware of having been born into a sinful situation without his consent:

> See, in guilt I was born,
> and in sin did my mother conceive me. (vs. 5)

The two insights are not contradictory. The world that surrounds us is tainted by mankind's age-old sinfulness. We absorb self-defeating and self-destructive habits of living from the people around us. But we do plunge into this ocean of sinfulness and make it our own, becoming willing victims and contributors to the system. Healing of sin will mean restoration of joy and gladness in the psalmist's life:

> Instil some joy and gladness into me,
> let the bones you have crushed rejoice again,
> hide your face from my sins,
> wipe out all my guilt. (vss. 8–9)
> Be my savior again, renew my joy. (vs. 12)

Conversion is not just a question of correcting one's conduct to bring it into line with proper norms. It involves nothing less than a change of heart:

> God, create a clean heart in me,
> put into me a new and constant spirit.
> (vs. 10)

The sinner cannot hope to buy forgiveness from God. All that the sinner has to offer is his own brokenness:

> Sacrifice gives you no pleasure,
> were I to offer holocaust,
> you would not have it.
> My sacrifice is this broken spirit,
> You will not scorn this crushed and broken heart.
> (vss. 16–17)

It is remarkable how lacking from biblical prayer of repentance are expressions of resolution or determination to do better in the future. These are not the prayers of the "broken" or "contrite" spirit. There are such prayers in the psalter, but they come out of a different experience; they are exultant cries of one who feels a God-given strength (cf. Ps. 26; 101). Psalms expressing repentance are mainly concerned with accepting responsibility and begging for healing.

Longing for God

A small but appealing group of psalms gives voice to a sense of the absence of God. Just as the temple in Jerusalem was, for some of the psalmists, the place of a vivid awareness of God's presence, so these psalms express a longing for God bound up with homesickness for Jerusalem and for the temple.

Psalms 42–43 were originally one psalm. Their unity is indicated by a common theme, and repetition of the refrain:

> Why are you so downcast, my soul,
>   why groan within me?
> Hope in God, I will praise him still,
>   my Savior and my God. (Ps. 42:5, 22; Ps. 43:5)

Thirsting is a common image for the experience of God's absence. The author of Psalm 42 compares his "throat" (*nephesh*) to a doe longing for running streams (vs. 1). He is in exile "in the country of Jordan and Mount Hermon" (vs. 6), which by our standards is not at all far from Jerusalem. He feels that he is on the verge of being overwhelmed by the mighty waters that lie below the earth and above the heavens. The "deep above" calls to the "deep below" and their chaotic waters threaten to join forces and engulf him:

> Deep is calling to deep,
> as your cataracts roar.
> Your torrents, and all your waves,
> swept over me. (Ps. 42:7)

The contempt of pagans who ask "Where is your God?" increases his distress, as do the attacks and calumnies of enemies in other psalms of desolation (Ps. 42:10). Nonetheless, the psalmist develops a sense of hope and certainty that he will again experience the presence of God in the temple (Ps. 43:3–4).

Psalm 63 also expresses thirst for God:

> My soul (throat, *nephesh*) is thirsting for you,
> my flesh is longing for you,
> a land parched, weary and waterless. (vs. 1)

The exile theme is not so strong as in Psalms 42–43, but the longing for God's presence is certainly bound up with longing for the Jerusalem temple (vs. 2). Verses 3–5 become immersed in a recollection of God's attributes and hence the poet moves into a sense of security that his longings will be fulfilled. Even present longing becomes suffused with joyful remembrance, and so becomes itself joyful:

> On my bed I think of you (i.e., he thinks of God even at night)
> I meditate on you all night long,
> for you have always helped me.
> I sing for joy in the shelter of your wings.
> My soul clings close to you,
> your right hand supports me. (vss. 6–8)

Enemies also feature in this psalm (vss. 9–10), and the king suddenly appears as rejoicing in the saving power of God. Perhaps this means that the whole psalm was meant as a prayer of the king. If so, it does not prevent us praying it in a personal way. Prayers for and of the king will be considered in the next chapter.

Psalm 137 vividly expresses the debilitating experience of homesickness, in this case experienced by the exiled Jews for Jerusalem. Present rejoicing seems impossible; they cannot "sing the song of the Lord on alien soil" (vs. 4). The last verses (vss. 8–9) express the bitterness and anger felt at those responsible for the sack of Jerusalem, and at the Edomites who took advantage of the fall of Jerusalem to take revenge for earlier humiliations they had suffered at the hands of the Jewish people (cf. Lam. 4:21). An Ezekiel or a Jeremiah could tell the people that the exile was brought on by their sin; the feeling of bitterness toward the immediate instruments of God's anger remained, just as we can have some awareness of our own sinful attitudes that alienate others, yet still feel bitterness toward them. Once more such sentiments can be expressed in prayer.

Psalm 61 combines prayer for defense against enemies (vss. 1–2), a prayer to be kept in God's presence (vs. 4) and a prayer for the king (vss. 6–7), which we shall consider again in the chapter following. Once again the poet is in exile:

> From the end of the earth I call to you,
> with sinking heart. (vs. 2)

Though his desire is mainly for God's protection, it is still bound up with nostalgia for the temple:

Let me stay in your Tent forever,
taking refuge in the shelter of your wings.
                              (vs. 4)

He refers twice to "vows" he has taken and wishes to fulfill (vss. 5, 8).
In keeping with Old Testament custom these would involve sacrifices
that he proposes to offer regularly in the temple.

It is not difficult to identify with the sentiments expressed in these
psalms—a sense of the absence of God leading to a thirst for him.
Sometimes we may find it possible to identify more completely with
their sentiments when we know the emptiness and loneliness that
come from being separated from well-loved places and surroundings
that formerly mediated the presence of God to us.

Conclusions

The wide range of emotions expressed in the psalms of desolation is
remarkable. Many of them are states of mind and heart that we tend
to fear as threats to our own well-being and our relationship with God.
Yet the basic rule of prayer exemplified in these psalms is not only
"Tell it like it is," but, more basic still, "Feel it like it is." Entering
fully into the painful and sometimes shameful emotions that agitate
us seems to be not only permissible but advisable. We can do this only
if we have a basic trust that our emotions need never overpower us
and lead to destructive acting out; in prayer we enter into our emotions in the presence of and in the company of God who holds the
waters of chaos at bay. Entering thus into our painful emotions we
discover that they are not, as we were inclined to fear, eternal and
boundless, but finite and bounded by an end. Looked at from the
outside, emotional storms look endless, and we fear to enter into them
because we have no assurance that we will ever come out. Entering
into them prayerfully shows us that this is not so, and tends to rob
them of their power to terrify.

It is remarkable that prayer in desolation tends to shade back into
prayer of exultation. There are prayers of unrelieved desolation, like
Psalms 88 and 39, but they are the exception rather than the rule.
Generally the psalmist lets himself feel the full weight of his present
desolation, only to find that, having depthed his suffering, he finds a
new source of peace and security (Lam. 3:55–56; Ps. 6:7–8; 28:5–6;

31:19–24; 55:16ff; 57:7ff; 109:30ff). There are other psalms where an awareness of present suffering and an awareness of the greatness of God alternate, almost struggling for supremacy. An example is Psalm 22, which cannot be accused of glossing over the reality of suffering, but still ends with an expression of confidence (vss. 22–31). Finally, there are psalms that give the merest nod to the present painful circumstances, only to move immediately into an awareness of God's greatness and propensity to save. One cannot really say that any one of these forms of prayer is "better" than others. Each is a reflection of a genuine prayer experience, and we can conclude that the experience of unrelieved distress is the exception rather than the rule. The willingness to include psalms that do express this exceptional experience shows that the Old Testament felt no need to suppress it, as though it would constitute a threat to some preconceived idea of how prayer should function.

This is not to say that entering into a painful storm of emotions cannot be frightening in the extreme. No one can absolutely guarantee that we will not find ourselves marooned in a sea of unending suffering. As the psalms themselves suggest by their practice of recalling past experience of God's mercies when the present looks grim, our own experiences can provide comfort for the fainthearted when the darkness looks impenetrable. But the proverb does say "There's always a first time," expressing some of the ingrained mistrust and cynicism that is endemic to human nature, and we shall probably persist in trying to chart a course around the problem areas in our lives until it becomes evident that it doesn't work, and that a dark patch in our lives, which we deliberately skirt, continues to exercise a baleful influence even when we do not allow it to burst upon us with full force. Any peace and contentment achieved by skirting the trouble spots, whistling as we pass the cemetery, is *felt* as hollow and ultimately unsatisfying. If we listen to our hearts we cannot be satisfied with it.

We have also noted that sometimes in prayer the psalmists disclaim responsibility for the suffering they are experiencing, and sometimes (and, one gets the impression, against a good deal of inner resistance) they accept a degree of personal responsibility. We have no right to claim that the psalms protesting innocence in the midst of suffering, like Psalms 7, 17, and 35, are "better" or "worse" than those like

Psalms 25 and 38 where the psalmist accepts responsibility. Nor can we really claim that the authors of the first kind of psalm "should have" ultimately arrived at a sense of personal responsibility like that of the authors of the second group. But the experience of these latter authors does suggest that in time of desolation the block to our progress through suffering to peace can at least sometimes be failure to recognize our own responsibility.

Against some rather fundamentalist understandings of the Scriptural doctrine on suffering, I maintain that pain is part of the natural order of things, just as pleasure is. The person who has no sensitivity to pain—and there are medical conditions that produce this effect—is ill equipped to cope with reality, incapable of distinguishing the destructive from what is health-giving. Pain was not invented by God as a punishment for sin; it is part of the equipment of the sensitive being. Human sinfulness did not create or even occasion pain, but it did wreck the human capacity to cope with pain and use it constructively. Instead of accepting pain as feeding us useful, perhaps vital, information about ourselves and the world around us, we flee it as an unmitigated evil and refuse to accept it into our scheme of things. We fight against it, rendering it still more painful and destructive by adding a discordant jangle of unnecessary emotion. Or, perversely, we cast the blame for pain on others—on God, or on our fellow human beings—while all the while we may be inflicting it upon ourselves.

Pain is neither to be avoided nor ignored—nor, for that matter, sought out. The psalms encourage us to enter into our pain, and to let it lead us where it will. It may conceivably be to a realization of the mysterious place of pain in our lives, just as Job realized that his otherwise inexplicable pain had a place in a far vaster and wiser scheme of things than he was capable of grasping, and the recognition itself was healing. Or it may lead us to the discovery that our pain is in fact self-inflicted and the consequence of freely adopted attitudes. Though we may not be able to change these attitudes at will, since we have never known any others, they are nonetheless our own, and for them we must accept responsibility. And this very acceptance is the beginning of healing.

Again, it is perhaps for the best that we can give no rule of thumb to judge whether or not suffering is self-inflicted—the consequence of our sinful choices and sinful attitudes. This would short-circuit the process and relieve us of the responsibility of discovering it for ourselves. It is only by entering into the desolation and letting the suffering be that we can experience it for what it is, and be led to recognize our responsibility for it or embrace it as a mysterious trial sent by God, accordingly as seems appropriate.

8

Messianic Psalms

There is a group of psalms that in one way or another are concerned with the Messiah. The word is familiar to Christians, since confession of Jesus of Nazareth as the Messiah or the "Christ" (the latter is simply a Greek word with the same meaning as the Hebrew word "Messiah") is central to Christianity. In fact it is so central that our view of what the Old Testament hoped for from the Messiah tends to be distorted. We imagine that the hope of the Messiah was equally as central to the Old Testament view of things as it is to our own. We imagine that the Old Testament expected as much of the Messiah as we expect of Jesus.

Furthermore, since Christian apologetes have traditionally attached great importance to "proving" to their own satisfaction that Jesus of Nazareth is the "Messiah" prophesied in the Old Testament, we imagine that the Old Testament existed simply to provide an Identikit picture of the Messiah, so that the Jewish people could welcome this one unique individual when he came. This perspective makes the Jewish people guilty of incredible blindness and hardness of heart in perversely refusing to accept Jesus, so clearly predicted in their sacred writings.

In fact the Old Testament was written in response to the vicissitudes of some two millennia of Jewish history. Its authors wrote primarily with the needs of their own time in view, though the fact that their works came to be treasured down through centuries indicates that they continued to speak to their readers long after the original occasion of writing or speaking had passed. Constant throughout is hope for the future. Even in the darkest hours of their history a hope that God would be with his people and ultimately save them survives. But not all hope is messianic, if we are to take the word seriously. "Messiah" (and the Greek "Christos" from which is derived our word "Christ") means "anointed one." In some circles, centered, naturally, in the southern kingdom with its loyalty to the house of David and strong feeling for Jerusalem, it was assumed that God's plans for his people would always include the monarchy as the instrument through which he ruled and blessed his people. Hope for salvation, which includes the king, the anointed one, is the one hope that can be called in the strict sense "messianic."

Especially at times of national crisis the hope is expressed that God will send an "anointed one" or king to see them through the hard times ahead. Sometimes, as in Amos 9:11–12, this is a vague hope that God will restore the glory of the house of David to what it was in David's time. In some of the more famous messianic prophecies (e.g. Is. 7–11) more detailed hopes for the expected king are expressed. Isaiah's hope was for a king to rescue the people from the threats of his own time, the mid-eighth century B.C. But his expectations were so glowing that they were never quite exhausted, and there remained a margin for hope which encouraged later generations to believe that the promise was not exhausted.

Hope is always limited in its vision of the future by experiences of the past. In fact, hope is formulated as a projection into the future of the good things experienced in the past, eliminating what has made the past less than perfect and exaggerating what has been experienced as good. The image of the future king who will be God's instrument in saving his people is modeled after the kings of the past, and is normally pictured with all the regal trappings of power. Just once, in Zechariah 9:9–10, the poet dares to conceive of a new kind of king, one who will combine kingly power with the resourcelessness and utter dependence on God that is characteristic of the poor in spirit:

> Rejoice heart and soul, daughter of Zion,
> Shout with gladness, daughter of Jerusalem!
> See now, your king comes to you.
> He is victorious, he is triumphant,
> humble, and riding on a donkey,
> on a colt, the foal of a donkey.

The regal features that were so much part of the traditional picture of the Messiah were totally lacking in Jesus of Nazareth. In fact, the gospels show us Jesus constantly under pressure to live up to other people's expectation of what the Messiah should be—and steadfastly refusing to do so. Jesus himself never explicitly claimed the title of "Messiah," and generally accepted it when it was bestowed on him by others only with reluctance; it was a title freighted with all sorts of meaning Jesus did not want to buy into. In the end, Jesus was a disappointment to those who expected him to show the traditional regal qualities of the Messiah. Ultimately his condemnation by the high priest (cf. Mk. 15:62–64) was probably not simply because he claimed to be the Son of God, one of the traditional titles granted to the king, but that he, powerless and abandoned by his followers, should insult God by agreeing that he was the ruler sent by God.

From earliest times "Messiah" was the favorite designation of Jesus among Christians. It may seem at first strange that this should be so, because Jesus himself was cool toward the title. But its popularity among Christians was probably due to the fact that it focused clearly on the special nature of Christianity. Only someone weaned from the nationalistic vision of salvation that was part of the Jewish ethos could accept the powerless Jesus of Nazareth as Messiah.

When we approach the messianic psalms, therefore, we are acutely aware that they can be read at two different levels. They can be read at the Jewish level of understanding—when they praise a king who fits the ordinary ancient Near Eastern pattern of kingship in many respects—or, if we want to apply them to Jesus, many of their features can be interpreted in a metaphorical way. We generally make this transposition without too much thought. But our appreciation of the uniqueness of Jesus and our understanding of the mysterious relationship between the longings of the human heart and their fulfillment will be deepened if we are aware of the paradox.

Some of the messianic psalms are in praise of the king, others are prayers for the king, and still others are prayers of the king for himself. We shall consider them in that order.

Praise of the king
In Psalm 2 the speaker is the king, but since the psalm is a triumphant proclamation of the standing of the divinely appointed king, it fits best into the first category. The psalm is for the occasion of a royal corona-

tion, the day on which the newly enthroned king can lay claim to the privileged title "Son of God":

> Let me proclaim Yahweh's decree;
> he has told me, "You are my son,
> today I have become your father." (vs. 7)

In the Old Testament the ordinary member of the chosen race very rarely, and then only in later books, lays claim to being "Son of God." The title is applied to the nation as a whole, personified as God's son (or daughter) (cf. Hos. 11:1–6; Ezek. 16), and the king (cf. 2 Sam. 7:14). The king has a divine mandate to rule over the nations—an act of faith in God's plans for his people, which historically never amounted to much on the stage of world politics. The poet imagines the nations sullenly muttering and rebellious, but God, triumphant and majestic in the heavens, laughs at their puny efforts to evade the decrees of his will:

> The one who sits in heaven laughs,
> Yahweh derides them.
> Then angrily he addresses them,
> in a rage he strikes them with panic,
> "This is my king, installed by me
> on Zion, my holy mountain." (vss. 4–6)

Acceptance of the divinely ordered decrees is "wisdom"—the fear of the Lord we considered earlier—and rebellion against it is the way to self-inflicted disaster:

> So now, you kings, learn wisdom,
> earthly rulers, be warned:
> serve Yahweh, fear him,
> tremble and kiss his feet,
> or he will be angry and you will perish,
> for his anger is very quick to blaze. (vss. 10–11)

Early Christian theology was not afraid to apply this picture of the king entering upon his "divine sonship" to Jesus' resurrection, when he was established "Son of God in power" (cf. Rom. 1:4; Heb. 5:5), although later theology has on the whole been reluctant to use language suggesting that Jesus was ever anything less than Son of God.

However, it is certainly at the resurrection that the New Testament sees Jesus entering upon the full exercise of his divine sonship and universal dominion. This is, for example, evident in the gospel of Matthew, where, in contrast to his earlier refusal to extend his ministry beyond the "lost sheep of the house of Israel" (cf. Mt. 15:24; 10:5–6), after the resurrection Jesus claims "All authority in heaven and earth is given to me" and gives his disciples a commission to preach the gospel to "every creature" (Mt. 28:19).

Psalm 45 is a song for a royal wedding, praising the royal groom and his consort in extravagant terms. The poet describes the king as champion of God's cause, ensured of a long reign, and excelling all his rivals. Verses 6–7 go so far as to address him in seemingly divine terms:

> Your throne, God, shall last forever and ever,
> your royal scepter is the scepter of integrity,
> virtue you love as much as you hate wickedness.
> This is why God, your God, has anointed you
> with the oil of gladness, above your rivals.

We have already seen that the title "god" can be given to human beings who share in Yahweh's function of ruling. The promise that his throne will last forever makes sense in the light of the hopes for David's dynasty, which was expected to last forever (cf. 2 Sam. 7:13). Christians will see these claims applying to Christ in a much more literal way than they ever applied to a historical king of Judah.

From Verse 10 to the end of the psalm, the poet turns his attention to the queen, whom he exhorts to forget her past and devote herself totally to her new husband. Her claim to fame will no longer be a distinguished ancestry, but the sons she will contribute to the royal line. Her greatness lies not so much in the past as in the future.

> Your ancestors will be replaced by sons,
> whom you will make lords of the whole world.
> (vs. 16)

All this can easily be applied to the church or to the Christian, whose greatness lies in being dedicated to Christ (2 Cor. 11:12) and who should look to the future rather than to the past as the place where greatness is to be achieved.

Of all the psalms in praise of the Messiah, Psalm 110 must be the most extravagant. Here the poet envisages the king enthroned at the right hand of God, lording it over his enemies (vss. 1–2, 5–6). Verse 3 is so obscure that no agreed interpretation of it can be offered; its obscurity does not prevent us understanding the rest of the psalm.

Verse 4 is something of a *tour de force*. Throughout the Near East it was usual for the king also to be the high priest, the chief cult functionary of the royal temple. The chosen race was unusual in that the priesthood was separate from the monarchy. In the south the two functions were the prerogatives of two different tribes. Priests were of the tribe of Levi, kings of the tribe of Judah. Psalm 110 uses Genesis 14:18–22 to claim that the king does possess a special kind of priesthood. The passage relates that Abraham was favorably received by and formed a pact with Melchizedek, king of Jerusalem, at that time still in the hands of the Canaanite tribe of the Jebusites.

The king of Jerusalem is, in accordance with ancient Middle Eastern custom, also the high priest, and his god is called "God most high" (*'El 'elyon*). Later generations supposed that "god most high" could only be Yahweh, having lost touch with the time when their land was peopled by pagans. In this little detail, then, the psalmist finds a link between priesthood and the throne. Could not the Davidic kings claim to be successors to this mysterious Melchizedek, king and priest in Jerusalem in pre-Davidic times, and therefore claim a priesthood, not the Levitical line, but "according to the line of Melchizedek."

The king, as described in Psalm 110, is also a mighty warrior. The final verse of the psalm attracts attention:

> He shall drink from the stream by the way,
> therefore he shall lift up his head. (vs. 7)

Almost instinctively one looks for a deeper meaning. Is this stream perhaps the God-given living water described in Jeremiah 2:13 or Ezekiel 47:1–12? Or is it the spring of Siloam, which gives water and life to the city of Jerusalem and becomes symbolic of the life-giving God of Israel (Is. 8)? Perhaps it is better to be content with a simpler understanding. This is part of the picture of the indefatigable warrior who, after wreaking the havoc described in verses 5–6, needs only to slake his thirst at a wayside stream to be ready for further exploits.

These warlike features of the psalm can be applied to Jesus in the same way as the warlike features of Psalm 2—with a vivid awareness that we are making metaphorical use of hopes that were originally taken in a much more literal sense. Psalm 110 also provides the author of the letter to the Hebrews with an Old Testament precedent for claiming that Jesus, first and foremost the Messiah of the tribe of Judah, also has a priestly function, despite his not being of the priestly tribe of Levi (Heb. 8–9).

Up to now it has been possible to view the psalms as expressions of deeply human longings, transcending the boundaries of time and culture. In the messianic psalms we may seem to have strayed into something much more distant from us. We have to assimilate an Old Testament conception of the "Messiah" that is rather foreign to our ways of thinking. Old Testament statements about the Messiah get transposed into highly theological statements about the nature of Christ. It sounds as though we are dealing with a history of ideas rather than with prayer of the heart.

Even these psalms, however, express something more than ideas. They express an ideal of a hero in which the psalmist rejoiced, and that he longed to see fulfilled. We can probably find in our hearts also something that lifts and exults in the triumphalist imagery. Somewhere in us, too, is a triumphalist ideal of human greatness based on power and imposed on others by force. We will quite likely find ourselves passionately committed to and lost in admiration of a triumphalist image of the Messiah, even if we transpose the triumphalism to the spiritual plane, and expect some kind of spiritual but glorious kingdom. We long to be saved, but we also long to dominate.

On the other hand, we may react to the picture of a triumphalist Messiah with repugnance, especially if it brings to the surface half-repressed fears of a Christ who somehow imprisons us in demands and restrictions. Such images need to be brought out into the light of God in prayer, and not simply pushed back into the depths as "wrong." They may not be the image of Christ authorized by faith, but pushed back into the depths they will never be transformed. They will remain an unrecognized obstacle to trust in Jesus, like the bogey man a child imagines under the bed but is too afraid to banish once for all by looking.

Even as Christians, a purification of our messianic hopes and images is necessary.

Prayers for the king

Psalm 89 grows out of the experience of having messianic expectations purified. We have already considered it as a striking example of honest prayer in desolation. It is the prayer of a person committed to the messianic ideal and messianic hopes at the time of the exile, which contradicted all that he had learned to hope. As happens so often in prayers of deep self-questioning, this psalm begins by stating faith in the very object of doubt—the steadfastness of Yahweh's love (vss. 1–15) and his power manifested in control of creation (vss. 9–12). It recalls in loving detail the unconditional promises of God to David and his descendants (vss. 19–37), which contrast so pitiably with the present circumstances that are described in detail (vss. 38–45). The prayer concludes with a plea for restoration (vss. 46–51). In a general way we can certainly identify with the disconcerting realization that God is not dealing with us in the way we hoped and expected he would. We may be able to identify a little more closely still with the psalm's sentiments if we dare admit that the Christ we come to know in the course of our life experience is different from the triumphant Christ we had expected to meet. This may well amount to a crisis of faith, but a crisis of faith is not to be kept out of our prayer. It may even lead us to a stronger and purified faith—if we can assimilate it into our prayer.

Psalm 72 is a prayer of petition for the king, though it quickly merges into an expression of confidence that the poet's hopes will be fulfilled. Verses 1–2 pray that God may share his own justice with the king, and in keeping with the Hebrew notion of justice we explored earlier, this will enable him to "uprightly defend the poorest, save the children of those in need, and crush their oppressors" (vs. 4; cf. vss. 12–13). If he participates in God's justice, the king will be unequivocally on the side of the downtrodden. He is expected to have a long reign, desirable in a good king to provide stability (vs. 5). His dominion will reach from sea to sea, and from the river (Nile) to the end of the earth (vs. 8); in particular, Egypt ("the beast") will be subject to him, as well as the kings of Tarshish (regularly regarded as the westernmost point of the world) and of the regions of fabled wealth to the south of Egypt (vss. 10–11). He will be loved and esteemed (vs. 15), and God's blessing will be evident even in the fertility of the land (vs. 16).

It would not be impossible, even today, to pray this psalm for rulers, even if the high hopes expressed might then begin to sound rather naive and unrealistic. But we can still apply a psalm like this to Jesus Christ. The exercise of his lordship is not yet complete, and the glowing picture of the blessings of his triumph is still a hope. We can pray Psalm 72 as an exercise in faith and hope in what this lordship will mean, and a prayer that it be brought to fulfillment. We sometimes need to strengthen our wavering faith that Jesus has the power to make all things new and unravel the seemingly inextricably tangled skein of human wickedness.

Psalm 20 can be similarly applied. It prays for triumph of the king in battle (vss. 1–5, 9) and expresses faith in his power to save (vss. 6–8). Verse 7 voices the trust in God and freedom from concern for material resources that is part of the Old Testament ideal:

> Some boast of chariots, some of horses,
> but we boast about the name of Yahweh our God.
> Theirs to crumple and fall,
> but we shall stand, and stand firm. (vss. 7–8)

The fact that we believe that God will infallibly complete the work of Christ and that the final victory is certain does not make it impossible for us to pray that this may be fulfilled, in much the same way as we believe that God's will must be done, yet still pray "Thy will be done." It is a human need to express the longings of our hearts, even if we are assured that God wants to fulfill the longings of the human heart (cf. Ps. 20:3). Psalm 21 takes up this theme and thanks God for granting the desires of the king's heart. While it is possible to pray for the fulfillment of God's plans as in Psalm 20, it is also possible to thank him for their fulfillment as in Psalm 21, depending on whether one is more aware of one side or the other of the Christian paradox of victory won yet not complete.

Prayers of the king

Many of the psalms of course are ascribed to King David but this convention, for the most part, does not contribute to or affect our personal use of them. Scholars have also speculated that the "I" who speaks in any psalm can usually be presumed to be the king. This is difficult to prove, and contributes little to the fruitful personal use of the psalms. We will do better to leave this kind of speculation aside, of interest to the scholar but of little significance for the person praying (even if he or she happens to be also a scholar).

Psalm 18 is a song of thanksgiving, and would fit into the category of prayer of exultation. However, it is clearly a prayer of the king, and his thanksgiving is for a successful reign:

> You deliver me from a people in revolt,
> you place me at the head of the nations,
> a people I did not know are now my servants,
> foreigners come wooing my favor.
> No sooner do they hear than they obey me,
> foreigners grow faint of heart,
> they come trembling out of their strongholds. (vss. 43–45)
> Yahweh saves his king again and again,
> displays his love for his anointed,
> for David and his heirs forever. (vs. 50)

The threat that he has successfully survived is described in the imagery of a flood of water (vss. 4–5), and in the coming of God to save, in terms that are now familiar: a thunderstorm driving back the waters after the pattern of Exodus:

> He bent the heavens and came down,
> a dark cloud under his feet;
> he mounted a cherub and flew,
> and soared on the wings of the wind.
> Darkness he made a veil to surround him,
> his tent a watery darkness, dense cloud,
> before him a flash enkindled hail and fiery embers,
> Yahweh thundered from heaven,
> the Most High let his voice be heard;
> He let his arrows fly and scattered them,
> launched his lightnings and routed them.
> The bed of the seas was revealed,
> The foundations of the world were laid bare,
> at your muttered threat, Yahweh,
> at the blast of your nostrils' breath. (vss. 9–15)

In verses 18–27 the king ascribes his success to his rightness of heart, raising the same kind of questions raised earlier in Psalm 66:18. The sense of being empowered by Yahweh to do great things is expressed in verses 27–48 under many images—many of them warlike.

Psalm 3 could be a prayer of the king, since it complains that "more and more are rebelling against me" (vs. 1), though other explanations of the phrase could be found. Psalm 144 begins with thanksgiving for success and victory that applies most naturally to a king:

> Blessed by Yahweh, my rock,
> who trains my hands for war,
> and my fingers for battle.
> My love, my bastion,
> my citadel, my savior,
> I shelter behind him, my shield,
> he makes nations submit to me. (vss. 1–2)

It then moves to petition (vss. 5–15), asking for freedom from alien oppression and prosperity.

Because these psalms are prayers of the king, it is tempting to think that we can pray them only in the person of Christ, identifying with and taking delight in his dominion over the nations. This is certainly a legitimate way of using them in a Christian setting. However, the psalms can be a powerful way of opening ourselves to dialogue with God if we, at least sometimes, dare to identify with the speaker. This involves casting ourselves in the role of a king—not a king recognized and legitimized by common consent, but a self-crowned king in our own univese. Few of us can claim to have actually been set at the head of a nation or given dominion over foreigners. But still fewer of us can claim to have renounced a desire to dominate. Even if we have cast ourselves in the powerless or victim role, which we may even imagine to be religiously sanctioned, the role may well be a subtle way of coping with life and bending our kingdom to our will. We can often dominate more effectively from a position of victimhood than by a drive for naked power. We can really treat it as an affront when the world will not accord us royal honors. If we bring our subtle satisfaction at the success of our cleverly disguised ploys for dominance over others to expression before God in the words of Psalm 18 or Psalm 144, or if we express to God our distress that others refuse to submit to our will in the words of Psalm 3, we can never look at them in quite the same way again.

In other psalms the fact that the king is the person praying is less obtrusive. Psalm 63 seems to be a prayer of the king; verse 10 sounds as though the person praying suddenly begins to speak of himself as "the king" who will rejoice at the fulfillment of the longings expressed earlier. It makes so little difference to the psalm it can be practically ignored. Psalm 89, the psalm of anguish at the downfall of the monarchy, could also be prayed by the humiliated king, since he identifies so closely with the fate of the monarchy as to pray "remember me" in verse 47. There are other ways of explaining this verse, but if it is a prayer of the king himself the anguish over the seeming failure of God's promises acquires still more personal overtones.

Psalm 101 also sounds like a prayer of the king. We have already remarked that some of the intentions expressed could easily be conceived by a private person (e.g., not listening to slanderers), but others only make sense as a plan of a person in authority (e.g., "banishing from the city of the Lord all who do evil" (vs. 8). These intentions may serve to reveal to us our unreal expectations of controlling the lives of others.

9

Hearing and Understanding the Word

Modern Scripture scholarship treats its subject with a familiarity and a clinical curiosity that can seem far removed from the reverent submission due to the Word of God. I have presumed to criticize some psalms as less than adequate expressions of the movement of the Spirit, or even suggested that sometimes they express attitudes which are inadequate, narrow, or shortsighted. At times I find myself asking if I have not made my own experience and conceptions my yardstick for understanding and measuring the Word of God. There is a long and revered tradition that regards faith as a readiness to accept the Word of God at its face value, no matter how outlandish or scandalous the surface meaning of the word may seem. Is not faith a readiness to lay aside human reasonings and questionings and completely and unreservedly submit to the infinite and sovereign wisdom of God, as expressed in his inspired Word?

Reverent acceptance of any word demands that we become totally involved in hearing that word, paying homage by putting at its service the entire range of our faculties of knowing and understanding. To assume too readily that I know the meaning of God's Word, and to commit myself unthinkingly to what I brashly assume its meaning to be, ultimately cheapens the notion of faith. So doing, I run the risk of never discovering the living and life-giving God who speaks, but simply rediscovering my own presuppositions and prejudices. Paying homage to my own ideas and preconceptions, I discover a God made in my own image and likeness.

Human beings, in their longing for security and ultimate certainty, are quick to settle for idols rather than discover the security in freedom that comes from knowing the living God. The Israelites, having tasted the unsettling freedom of the desert, were willing to exchange it for the comfortable servitude they had known in Egypt. An idol seems more comforting than the real thing. An idol holds no mysteries, we understand it through and through; it is, after all, our own creation. An idol confronts us with no reminders of our finiteness, since it is finite like ourselves. It is less disturbing than the wild and overwhelming reality. An idol does not prompt the soul-searing, though healing, realization that "I am lost; I am a man of unclean lips, and I live among a people of unclean lips, and my eyes have seen the Lord, Yahweh Sabaoth" (Is. 6:5). So we enter, willingly though unwittingly, into a conspiracy to defend our idols.

What passes for faith then becomes commitment to an image made in our own image and likeness. Its counterfeit nature shows in its effects. It does not, as Jesus promises the truth will do, "set us free" (cf. Jn. 8:32). Deep down somewhere we sense that our idol cannot stand the light of day or the breath of fresh air, and, not wishing to see it crumble to dust before our eyes, we grant it privileged status, housing it in a temple we forbid ourselves to enter. A Jacob, or a Job, or a Jeremiah, who dares to wrestle with God, pays him more genuine homage than Ahaz, who "will not ask and will not tempt God" (Is. 7.12).

Faith is not a beleaguered virtue, assailed by hostile reality from without, and sabotaged by human powers of inquiry and knowing from within. A solid faith faces reality in the serene confidence that it is in touch with truth which will enable it to make sense of reality, or live with mystery when mystery remains. Faith is aware of the limitations of its own knowledge.

Listening is neither a totally active nor a totally passive operation. In listening one attempts to lay aside any presuppositions about what will or must be said, but we do not lay aside our rational nature, our powers of inquiry and curiosity, our capacity to question, our past. Only by drawing upon all our human, and God-given, powers of inquiry do we do justice to the Word and treat it with the seriousness it deserves.

Christians formerly read the Scriptures on the assumption that

God's Word somehow participated in the timelessness of God himself. They presumed that it was addressed directly to themselves, couched in the language that was congenial to them, in the thought categories of their own culture and age, which were for the most part the only ones they realized existed. Consequently they tended to hear only confirmation of their own culturally conditioned formulation of what faith was all about. Wherever cultural differences obtruded so as to create unavoidable difficulties in finding an acceptable Christian sense in the text, a deeper allegorical meaning was claimed.

Modern Scripture scholarship is colored by a keen awareness of the unstoppable flow of history in which all human events are located. God's Word is always, in the first instance, a "word for its time." It is heard in and through the human struggle to make sense of life and experience, in and through presuppositions derived from a cultural and ethnic background, shifts of thought prompted by crises of history, and the occasional flash of genial insight. Listening to the Word, the scholar hears echoes of all these influences. And reacting to centuries of unawareness of those influences, the scholar tends to stress above all the strangeness and foreignness of the biblical world of thought. He or she sometimes seems to take almost perverse delight in stressing what separates the modern Christian from the biblical authors. The non-scholars can be forgiven for feeling that the bible has been taken away from them.

I believe, however, that by opening myself as fully as possible to the word of the biblical author, I become aware of something more than differences. I share with the biblical author a common humanity. The reality that we face is, under many differences, identically structured, and at the basis of the reality we both experience is God.

The scholar in me is less assured when I try to penetrate this deeper level. So long as I confine myself to analyzing and explaining the written text, or describing the society and thought patterns of biblical times, I can strive for objectivity. I can support my claims by objective arguments. Better still, I can hide myself behind a learned apparatus of arguments and footnotes. Objectivity and impersonal detachment are ideals to be striven for. But once I venture to touch the underlying experience of which even the most eloquent word is an inadequate expression, I find myself driven back on personal testimony. I no longer have the comfort of appealing to textual, grammatical, or historical proofs. I must reveal something of myself and my own experience.

If we let the psalms lead us into the sometimes bewildering and frightening realm of the heart, we will, I believe, eventually discover there a still point beyond the storms and turmoil where a mysterious life-giving force is at work. I do not believe that we, children of a technological society, are bereft of this or incapable of getting in touch with it, but where former ages were ready to trust that they were in contrast with some transcendent force and only too ready to call it "God," modern technology has taught us to be cautious, not to say skeptical, about ultimate explanations. But I believe that if we take that experience seriously, accept it with reverence, and let it lead us where it will, we are responding to the God who inspired the psalmists.

Index of Psalms

66	82-84, 107, 160	108	104-106
67	63	109	98, 100, 102, 122, 148
68	44-45, 79	110	156-157
69	99-100, 115-116	111	80-81, 119-120
70	116	112	90-91
71	116	113	71
72	40, 79, 158-159	114	44
73	81, 124-126	115	74, 108-109
74	45, 109-110	116	77-78
75	81, 120	117	69
76	71-72	118	85
77	48, 109-111	119	92-94
78	42-43, 46	120	116
79	107, 110-111	121	77
80	104-105	122	65
81	134-135	123	116
82	73, 123, 135	124	44
83	106	125	65
84	65	126	46
85	106-108	127	81-82
86	114, 117	128	91
87	66	129	100
88	39, 44, 114-115, 147	130	78, 143
89	39-40, 44, 46-47, 109-111, 158, 162	131	29, 86
		132	46
90	128-129, 131-132	133	65-66, 94
91	76	134	87
92	76	135	41-42
93	61	136	40-41
94	123	137	146
95	73-74, 78-79	138	78
96	78-79	139	62-63
97	79-80	140	100
98	71	141	116
99	80	142	116
100	71	143	116, 143
101	94, 162	144	109, 161
102	74, 111-112	145	69-70, 72, 80
103	77, 79, 83	146	72
104	5, 58, 60-62	147	72
105	37-39	148	72
106	37-42, 44	149	72
107	51-52	150	40, 72-73